START CROCHET

START CROCHET

ALL YOU NEED TO KNOW TO CREATE BEAUTIFUL CROCHETED PIECES

Jan Eaton

APPLE

QUARTO BOOK

First published in the United Kingdom
by the Apple Press
Sheridan House, 112–116a Western Road
Hove, East Sussex BN3 1DD

www.apple-press.com

Copyright © 2004 by Quarto Plc

ISBN 1-8409-418-7

QUAR.CRBA

Conceived, designed and produced by
Quarto Publishing plc
The Old Brewery
6 Blundell Street
London N7 9BH

Project Editor **Paula McMahon**
Art Editor and Designer **Elizabeth Healey**
Assistant Art Director **Penny Cobb**
Copy Editor **Sue Viccars**
Photographer **Colin Bowling**
Illustrators **Coral Mula, Jennie Dooge**
Proof readers **Alison Leach, Hazel Williams**
Indexer **Pamela Ellis**

Art Director **Moira Clinch**
Publisher **Piers Spence**

Manufactured by Universal Graphics, Singapore
Printed by Star Standard Industries Pte Ltd,
Singapore

Contents

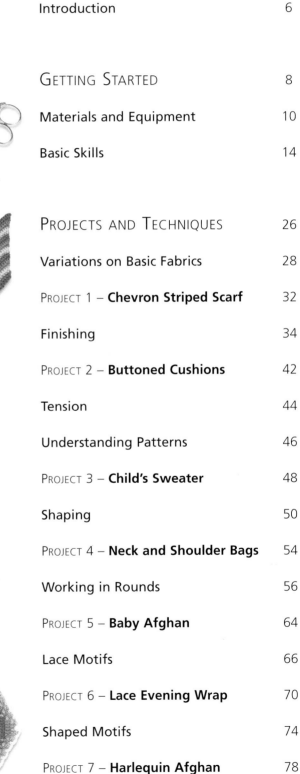

INTRODUCTION

CROCHET IS KNOWN THROUGHOUT THE WORLD: It is worked in countries from Europe to North and South America, Scandinavia to China, and is one of the oldest and most fascinating ways of creating a fabric with yarn. It's easy to produce wonderful fabrics using a continuous length of yarn and a hook, and the results can vary from gossamer-fine and lacy to soft, chunky, or textured. Once you have the hang of holding hook and yarn comfortably, the basic techniques of crochet are surprisingly easy to master, and all crochet forms, no matter how intricate they look at first, are based on a small number of stitches that are very easy to learn.

This book guides you through the building blocks of the craft of crochet. Begin by learning how to make a foundation chain (the equivalent of the knitter's cast on) and progress through the basic stitches and skills. Once you're confident with the basics, learn how to work different stitch patterns, work motifs in the round in a range of shapes and sizes, and learn how to work filet crochet. Work through the book with hook and yarn in hand, trying out the techniques and stitches, which lead you in easy steps through the learning process in a logical manner.

It's a good idea to make test pieces as you progress. You can build up your own practical crochet library, by keeping your test pieces in a box or file, labelling each one with information you may later need to refer to, including yarn type and colour, hook size and any other relevant details. This is a useful habit to

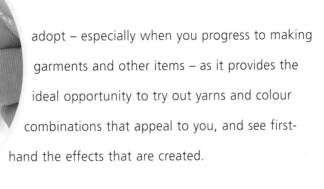

adopt – especially when you progress to making garments and other items – as it provides the ideal opportunity to try out yarns and colour combinations that appeal to you, and see first-hand the effects that are created.

When you're ready to move on to making the projects, tackle the ones you like in the order they appear in the book to ensure that you understand the necessary techniques. The projects are varied, starting with the simplest one and working up to more complicated designs, and will give you the opportunity to practise your new skills and make stylish and unusual garments, accessories and home furnishings. They have been designed to be adaptable to changing fashions in yarns and colours, and tips and swatches are included on how to make creative yet simple changes to the patterns and substitute individual colour choices to echo your own tastes.

Today's crocheter can be adventurous in choice of yarn as there's a wealth of modern and traditional yarns to be found both in shops and through the mail-order resources of the Internet. Old favourites such as pure wool spun in the Shetland Isles and strong, cotton yarns are joined by luxury pure silks, fine metallics and easy-care yarns made from child-friendly synthetic fibres. The range of hooks has widened over the last few years too – at one time you could only buy hooks made in your own country, but now American, British and European hooks are widely available.

GETTING STARTED

In this section you will find everything you need to know about starting to crochet, including how to choose hooks, information about the different fibres and yarns now available, and clear step-by-step instructions on how to work the basic stitches and techniques. The skills you need to learn are fully described and illustrated: how to work a foundation chain, how to construct the stitches, how to use turning chains to turn correctly at the end of a row, how to fasten off the yarn and deal with the yarn ends. These skills provide the basis of all forms of crochet and once you have learned, practised, and become familiar with the different stitches and techniques, you will be equipped to tackle your first project. Remember that practice makes perfect!

8

MATERIALS AND EQUIPMENT

Crochet is one of the easiest crafts to take up because you need very little initial equipment: just a ball of yarn and a crochet hook. Yarns for crochet come in a wide variety of materials, weights, colours and price ranges and it's important to choose the right yarn to suit your project. Other accessories (page 13), such as pins and sharp scissors, are useful and relatively inexpensive. Keep your crochet projects clean and dust-free by storing them in a fabric bag (a clean pillowcase is ideal), but avoid plastic because its static cling attracts dust and dirt that will transfer to your yarn.

Mohair

Wool

YARNS

Yarns are usually made by spinning different types of fibres together. The fibres may be natural materials obtained from animals or plants, for example wool or cotton, or they can be man-made fibres such as nylon or acrylic. Yarns may be made from one fibre or combine a mixture of two or three different ones in varying proportions. Several fine strands of yarn (called "plies") are often twisted together to make thicker weights of yarn. Novelty yarns such as tweeds and other textured yarns combine several strands of differing weights and textures twisted together. Metallics and ribbon yarns are constructed by knitting very fine yarn into tubes and giving them a rounded or flattened appearance. As a general rule, the easiest yarns to use for crochet, especially

Silk/Cotton

Silk

for a beginner, have a smooth surface and a medium or tight twist.

Yarn is sold by weight, rather than by length, although the packaging of many yarns now includes length per ball as well as other information. It is usually packaged into balls, although some yarns may come in the form of hanks or skeins which need to be wound by hand into balls before you can begin to crochet. The most common ball size is 50 g (1¾ oz) and the length of yarn in the ball will vary from yarn to yarn depending on thickness and fibre composition.

ANIMAL FIBRES

Wool is the most commonly used natural fibre because it is soft, warm to wear, relatively inexpensive and keeps its shape well. Woollen

yarns are spun from the shorn fleeces of sheep – other, more expensive animal fibres include mohair and cashmere (from goats) and angora (from angora rabbits), and are shorn or combed from the animal before being spun into yarn. Woollen yarns (or blended yarns with a high proportion of wool) feel nice to crochet with as they have a certain amount of stretch, making it easy to push the point of the hook into each stitch. Some yarns made from pure wool have to be laundered carefully by hand, although many are now treated to make them machine washable. Silk, spun from the unwound cocoons of the silkworm, is also a natural product. Silk yarn – like wool – is a good insulator, and has a delightful lustre, although it has less resilience and is much more expensive.

SYNTHETIC FIBRES

Acrylic, nylon, polyester and other synthetic fibres are manufactured from coal and petroleum products and are often made to resemble natural fibres. Yarns made wholly from synthetic fibres are usually less expensive and, although they are stable, machine washable, and don't shrink, they can lose their shape when heat is applied. The best solution is to choose a yarn where a small or equal proportion of synthetic fibres has been combined with a natural fibre such as wool or cotton.

VEGETABLE PRODUCTS

Both cotton and linen are derived from plants and are popular choices for summer garments as well as home furnishings. Crochet fabric made from cotton is durable and cool to wear, but pure cotton may lack resilience and is often blended with other fibres. Pure cotton and linen yarns are also rather prone to shrinkage. Rayon (viscose), a plant-based, man-made material, is soft and slightly shiny, and because it lacks elasticity it is usually combined with other fibres.

Cotton

YARN TYPES & WEIGHTS

Yarns are available in a range of weights varying from very fine to very bulky. Although each weight of yarn is described by a specific name, as shown in the samples to the right, there may actually be a lot of variation in the thicknesses when yarns are produced by different manufacturers or in different countries.

extra chunky

chunky

aran wool

Aran

4ply

aran cotton

double knitting

4ply mercerized cotton

aran acrylic

viscose rayon

linen/viscose

metallic/viscose

metallic

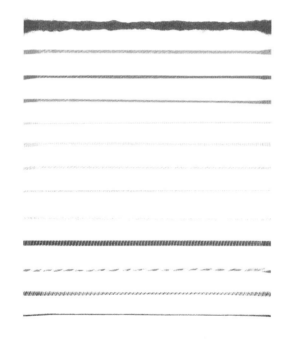

USEFUL HOOK/YARN COMBINATIONS

4ply (sport weight) 2.5–3.5 mm (B–E)
DK (double knitting) 3.5–4.5 mm (E–G)
Aran (worsted weight) 5–6 mm (I–J)

METRIC/US EQUIVALENTS

28 g = 1 oz
57 g = 2 oz
50 g = 1¾ oz
100 g = 3½ oz
2.5 cm = 1 in.
10 cm = 4 in.
91.4 cm = 1 yd
1 m = 39½ in.

CROCHET HOOKS

Crochet hooks are available in a wide range of sizes, shapes and materials. The most common sorts of hooks used for working with the types of yarn covered in this book are made from aluminium or plastic. Small sizes of steel hooks are also made for working crochet with very fine cotton yarns. (This type of fine work is known as thread crochet.) Some brands of aluminium and steel hooks have plastic handles to give a better grip (often called "soft touch" handles) and make the work easier on the fingers. Hand-made wooden and horn hooks are also available, many featuring decorative handles.

There appears to be no standardization of hook sizing between manufacturers. The points and throats of different brands of hooks often vary in shape which affects the size of stitch they produce.

Hook sizes are quoted differently in Europe and the United States and some brands of hooks are labelled with more than one type of numbering. Choosing a hook is largely a matter of personal preference and will depend on various factors such as hand size, finger length, weight of hook and whether you like the feel of aluminium or plastic in your hand.

The hook sizes quoted in pattern instructions are a very useful guide, but you may find that you need to use smaller or larger hook sizes, depending on the brand, to achieve the correct tension for a pattern. The most important thing to consider when choosing a hook is how it feels in your hand and the ease with which it works with your yarn. When you have found your perfect brand of hook, it's useful to buy a range of several different sizes. Store your hooks in a clean container – you can buy a fabric roll with loops to secure the hooks, or use a zipped pouch such as a cosmetic bag.

Throat *Thumb rest* *Shank*

Point

Aluminium and resin hooks

Comparative crochet hook sizes (from smallest to largest)

Steel			Aluminum or Plastic		
UK	METRIC (MM)	US	UK	METRIC (MM)	US
6	0.60	14	14	2.00	
5½		13	13		
5	0.75	12	12	2.50	B
4½		11	11	3.00	C
4	1.00	10	10		D
3½		9	9	3.50	E
3	1.25	8	8	4.00	F
2½	1.50	7	7	4.50	G
2	1.75	6	6	5.00	H
1½		5	5	5.50	I
1	2.00	4	4	6.00	J
1/0		3	2	7.00	K
2/0	2.50	2			
3/0	3.00	1			
		0			
	3.50	00			

ADDITIONAL EQUIPMENT

Tapestry needle

MARKERS

Split rings or shaped loops made from brightly coloured plastic can be slipped onto your crochet to mark a place on a pattern, to indicate the beginning row of a repeat, and to help with counting the stitches on the foundation chain.

TAPESTRY NEEDLES

Tapestry needles have blunt points and long eyes and are normally used for counted thread embroidery. They come in a range of sizes and are used for weaving in yarn ends and for sewing pieces of crochet together. Very large blunt-pointed needles are often labelled as "yarn needles". You may also need a selection of sewing needles with sharp points for applying crochet braid, edging or border to fabric.

PINS

Glass-headed rustproof pins are the best type to use for blocking (pages 34–35). Plastic-headed or pearl-headed pins can be used for pinning crochet and for cold-water blocking, but don't use this type for warm-steam blocking as the heat of the iron will melt the plastic heads. Quilters' long pins with fancy heads are useful when pinning pieces of crochet together as the heads are easy to see and won't slip through the crochet fabric.

TAPE MEASURE

Choose one that shows both centimeters and inches on the same side and replace when it becomes worn or frayed as this means it will probably have stretched and become inaccurate. A 30 cm (12 in.) metal or plastic ruler is also useful for measuring tension swatches.

Sharp scissors

ROW COUNTER

A knitter's row counter will help you keep track of the number of rows you have worked, or you may prefer to use a notebook and pencil.

SHARP SCISSORS

Choose a small, pointed pair to cut yarn and trim off yarn ends.

PLASTIC RINGS

These come in a variety of sizes and are used as foundations for making buttons. Don't use metal rings for button foundations as they may rust when a garment is laundered.

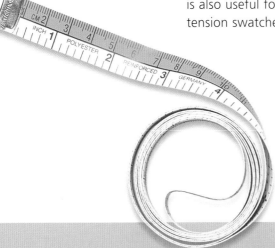

Tape measure

Quilters' pins

Basic Skills

To begin practising crochet, choose a smooth woollen yarn of double knitting or 4ply weight and a compatible hook size. Woollen yarn has a certain amount of "give" and is very easy to wo0rk with when you're a beginner. You can find more information on hooks and yarns on pages 10–12.

The foundation chain is the equivalent of casting on in knitting and it's important to make sure that you have made the required number of chains for the pattern you are going to work. The front of the chain looks like a series of "V" shapes or little hearts, while the back of the chain forms a distinctive "bump" of yarn behind each "V" shape. You can count the stitches on either the front or back of the chain, whichever you find easier. When counting a long foundation chain, it's a good idea to slip a ring marker into the chain to mark every 20 or 30 stitches. This will make it easier to check that you have worked the correct number.

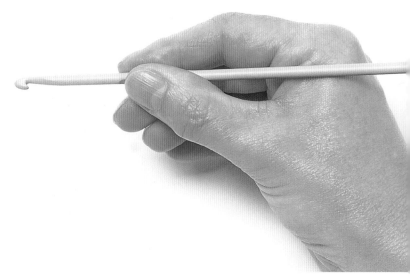

HOLDING THE HOOK

This is the most widely used way of holding the hook – as if it were a pen. Centre the tips of your right thumb and forefinger over the flat section of the hook.

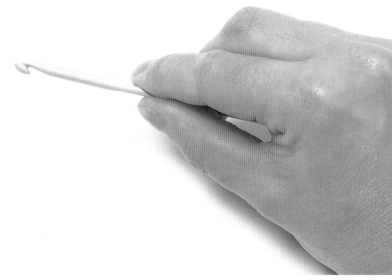

An alternative way is to grasp the flat section of the hook between your right thumb and forefinger as if you were holding a knife.

HOLDING THE YARN

To control the yarn supply, loop the short end of the yarn over your left forefinger and take the yarn coming from the ball loosely round the little finger on the same hand to tension it. Use your middle finger to help hold the work as you crochet.

This is a similar position which also leaves the middle finger free to hold the work. The yarn is tensioned round the ring finger of the left hand.

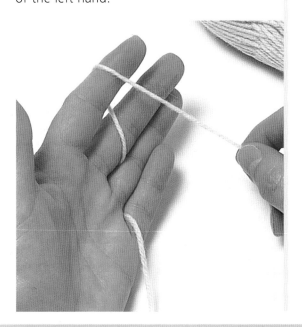

MAKING A SLIP KNOT

STEP 1
With about 15 cm (6 in.) of the end of the yarn at the left, loop the yarn round your right forefinger.

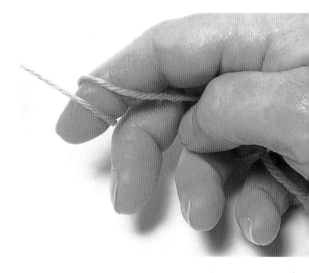

STEP 2
Carefully slip the loop off your finger. Holding the loop in your right hand, push a loop of the short end through the first loop.

STEP 3
Insert the hook into the second loop. Gently pull the short end of the yarn to tighten the loop round the hook and complete the slip knot.

STEP 1
Holding the hook with the slip knot in your right hand and the yarn in your left, wrap the yarn over the hook. This is known as yarn over or yarn over hook and, unless otherwise instructed, always wrap the yarn over the hook in this way.

STEP 2
Draw the yarn through to make a new loop and complete the first chain stitch.

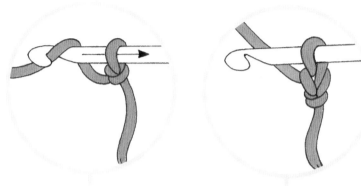

STEP 3
Repeat this step, drawing a new loop of yarn through the loop on the hook until the chain is the required length. Move up the thumb and forefinger that are grasping the chain after every few stitches to keep the tension even. When counting the chains, count each V-shaped loop on the front of the chain as one chain stitch (except for the loop on the hook which is not counted).

You may find it easier to turn the chain over and count the stitches on the back of the chain.

STEP 1
Now that you have made your foundation chain, you're ready to work the first row of stitches of your pattern into it. There are different places to insert the hook into the chain, but this way is easiest for the beginner. Holding the chain with the front facing you, insert the hook into the top loop of each chain. Although this gives rather a loose edge to a piece of crochet, it's ideal when an edge finish (pages 37–39) is to be worked.

STEP 2
To make a stronger, neater edge which can stand alone (without an edge finish being needed), turn the chain so the back of it is facing you. Work the first row of stitches of your pattern, inserting the hook into the "bump" at the back of each chain stitch.

TURNING CHAINS

When working crochet in rows or rounds, you will need to work a specific number of extra chains at the beginning of each row or round. The extra chains are needed to bring the hook up to the correct height for the particular stitch you will be working next. When the work is turned at the end of a straight row, the extra chains are called a turning chain, and when they are worked at the beginning of a round, they are called a starting chain.

TURNING CHAINS AND STITCH HEIGHT

The list below shows the correct number of chain stitches needed to make a turn for each stitch. If you have a tendency to work chain stitches very tightly, you may need to work an extra chain in order to keep the edges of your work from becoming too tight.

Double crochet stitch – 1 chain to turn
Half treble crochet stitch – 2 chains to turn
Treble crochet stitch – 3 chains to turn
Double treble crochet stitch – 4 chains to turn

Usually, the turning or starting chain is counted as the first stitch of the row, except when working double crochet where the single turning chain is ignored. For example, 3 ch (counts as 1 tr) at the beginning of a row or round means that the turning or starting chain contains three chain stitches and these are counted as the equivalent of one treble crochet stitch. A turning or starting chain may be longer than the number required for the stitch, and in that case counts as one stitch plus a number of chains. For example, 5 ch (counts as 1 tr, 2 ch) means that the turning or starting chain is the equivalent of one treble crochet stitch plus two chain stitches.

At the end of the row or round, the final stitch is usually worked into the turning or starting chain worked on the previous row or round. The final stitch may be worked into the top chain of the turning or starting chain or into another specified stitch of the chain.

BASIC STITCHES

WORKING A SLIPSTITCH (SL ST)

Slipstitch is rarely used to create a crochet fabric on its own. It is normally used to join rounds of crochet and to move the hook and yarn across a group of existing stitches. To work a slipstitch into the foundation chain, insert the hook from front to back under the top loop of the second chain from the hook. Wrap the yarn over the hook and draw it through both the chain and the loop on the hook. One loop remains on the hook and one slipstitch has been worked.

WORKING A DOUBLE CROCHET STITCH (DC)

STEP 1
To work a row of double crochet stitches into the foundation chain, insert the hook from front to back under the top loop of the second chain from the hook. Wrap the yarn over the hook and draw it through the first loop, leaving two loops on the hook.

STEP 2
To complete the stitch, wrap the yarn over the hook and draw it through both loops on the hook. Continue in this way along the row, working one double crochet stitch into each chain.

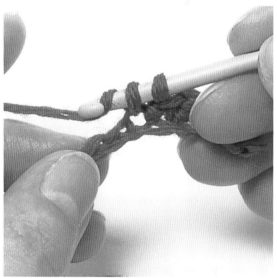

STEP 3
At the end of the row, turn and work one chain for the turning chain. (Remember that this chain does not count as a stitch.) Insert the hook from front to back under both loops of the first double crochet at the beginning of the row. Work a double crochet stitch into each stitch of the previous row, being careful to work the final double crochet stitch into the last stitch of the row below, but not into the turning chain.

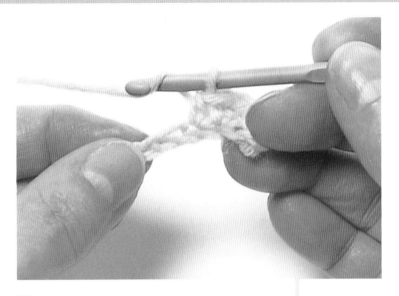

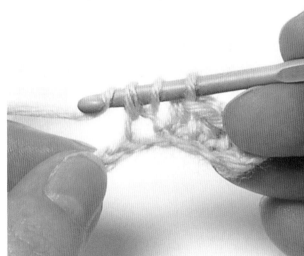

WORKING A HALF TREBLE CROCHET STITCH (HTR)

STEP 1 To work a
half treble crochet stitch,
wrap the yarn over the hook
and insert the hook from
front to back into the work.
(If you are at the beginning
of the first row, insert hook
under the top loop of the
third chain from the hook.)

STEP 2 Draw the yarn
through the chain, leaving three loops
on the hook. Wrap the yarn over the
hook and draw through all three
loops on the hook. One loop remains
on the hook and one half treble
crochet stitch has been worked.

STEP 3 Continue along the row,
working one half treble crochet stitch into
each chain. At the end of the row, work two
chains for the turning chain and turn.

STEP 4
Missing the first half treble crochet stitch at the beginning of the row, wrap the yarn over the hook, insert the hook from front to back under both loops of the second stitch on the previous row, and work a half treble crochet stitch into each stitch made on the previous row.

STEP 5
At the end of the row, work the last stitch into the top of the turning chain.

WORKING A TREBLE CROCHET STITCH (TR)

STEP 1
To work a treble crochet stitch, wrap the yarn over the hook and insert the hook from front to back into the work. (If you are at the beginning of the first row, insert the hook under the top loop of the fourth chain from the hook.)

Draw the yarn through the chain, leaving three loops on the hook.

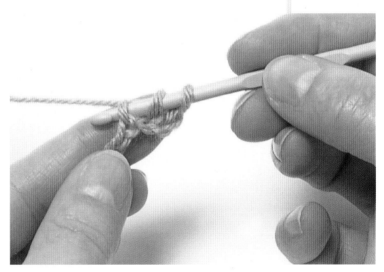

STEP 2
Wrap the yarn over the hook.

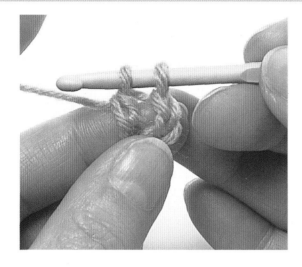

STEP 3
Draw the yarn through the first two loops on the hook. Two loops remain on the hook.

STEP 4
Wrap the yarn over the hook.

STEP 5
Draw the yarn through the two loops on the hook. One loop remains on the hook and one treble crochet stitch has been worked.

STEP 6
At the end of the row, work three chains for the turning chain and turn. Missing the first treble crochet stitch at the beginning of the row, wrap the yarn over the hook, insert the hook from front to back under both loops of the second stitch on the previous row, and work a treble crochet stitch into each stitch made on the previous row. At the end of the row, work the last stitch into the top of the turning chain.

Working a double treble crochet stitch (DTR)

STEP 1 To work a double treble crochet stitch, wrap the yarn over the hook twice. Insert the hook from front to back into the work. (If you are at the beginning of the first row, insert the hook under the top loop of the fifth chain from the hook.) Wrap the yarn over the hook and draw through, leaving four loops on the hook. Wrap the yarn over the hook.

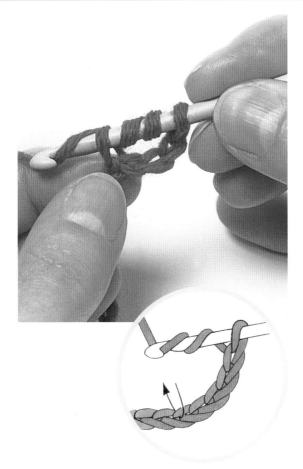

STEP 2 Draw through two loops (three loops on the hook), wrap again, draw through two loops (two loops on the hook). Wrap again and draw through the remaining two loops. Repeat along the row. At the beginning of every row, work four turning chains and insert the hook into the second stitch of the row. At the end of every row, work the last stitch into the top of the turning chain.

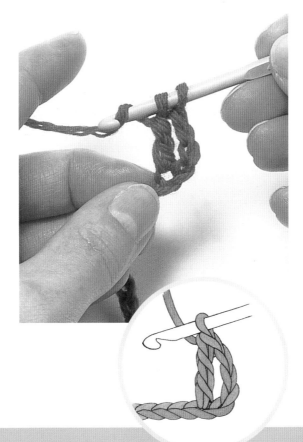

FABRICS MADE FROM BASIC STITCHES

DOUBLE CROCHET

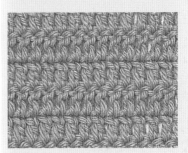

TREBLE CROCHET

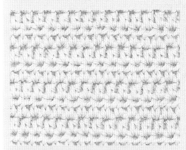

HALF TREBLE CROCHET

DOUBLE TREBLE CROCHET

Working into the front of a stitch

It's usual to work crochet stitches under both loops of the stitches made on the previous row. By working under one loop, either the back or the front, the remaining loop becomes a horizontal bar. To work into the front of a row of stitches, insert the hook under only the front loops of the stitches on the previous row.

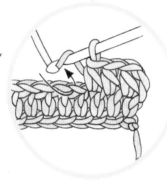

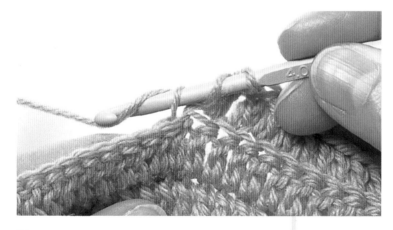

Working into the back of a stitch

Working into the back of the stitch creates a strongly ridged fabric. To work into the back of a row of stitches, insert the hook under only the back loops of the stitches on the previous row.

Fastening off yarn

STEP 1 To fasten off the yarn at the end of a piece of crochet, cut the yarn 15 cm (6 in.) from the last stitch. Work one chain stitch with the yarn end and pull the yarn end through the chain stitch with the hook.

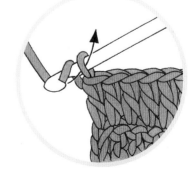

Gently pull the yarn end to tighten the chain stitch and weave the end in on the wrong side of the work (see below).

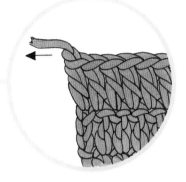

WEAVING A YARN END AT TOP EDGE

To weave a yarn end in at the top of the work, thread the end in a large tapestry needle. Weave the end through several stitches on the wrong side of the work. Trim the remaining yarn.

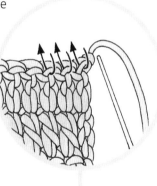

WEAVING A YARN END ALONG LOWER EDGE

To weave a yarn end in along the lower edge, thread the end in a tapestry needle and draw it through several stitches on the wrong side of the work. Trim the remaining yarn.

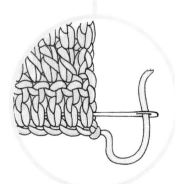

PROJECTS AND TECHNIQUES

ONCE YOU ARE CONFIDENT WORKING THE STITCHES AND TECHNIQUES OF CROCHET, IT'S TIME TO LEARN

HOW TO PUT THESE SKILLS INTO PRACTICE AND MASTER THE MORE ADVANCED TECHNIQUES. THIS

SECTION COVERS MANY VARIED TOPICS FROM UNDERSTANDING PATTERNS AND ABBREVIATIONS, MAKING

AND MEASURING TENSION SAMPLES, SHAPING, MAKING SEAMS AND EDGE FINISHES (INCLUDING

BUTTONHOLES AND BUTTON LOOPS), WORKING IN ROUNDS, MAKING AND JOINING COLOURFUL CROCHET

MOTIFS IN DIFFERENT SHAPES AND SIZES, WORKING ATTRACTIVE LACE AND TEXTURED STITCHES, FILET

CROCHET AND ADDING FINISHING TOUCHES SUCH AS EDGINGS, BORDERS, CORDS AND BUTTONS.

EACH TOPIC IS FULLY EXPLAINED AND ILLUSTRATED WITH STEP-BY-STEP PHOTOGRAPHIC SEQUENCES

BACKED UP WITH ILLUSTRATIONS.

YOU CAN SHOW OFF YOUR NEW-FOUND SKILLS BY MAKING A SERIES OF DELIGHTFUL PROJECTS.

THESE BEGIN WITH THE SIMPLEST ONE (CHEVRON STRIPED SCARF, PAGES 32–33) AND BUILD ON THE

KNOWLEDGE YOU HAVE GAINED UNTIL THE FINAL, MOST ELABORATE DESIGN (WINTER JACKET, PAGES

122–125). BY WORKING THROUGH THE BOOK IN ORDER, YOU WILL FIND THAT EACH PROJECT USES

THE TECHNIQUES ALREADY LEARNED AND BY THE END YOU WILL HAVE ACQUIRED ALL THE BASIC SKILLS

YOU NEED TO PURSUE THIS FASCINATING, ADDICTIVE AND CREATIVE CRAFT.

VARIATIONS ON BASIC FABRICS

The easiest way of changing a basic crochet fabric such as one worked in rows of treble crochet stitches is to begin to introduce more colours. Simple horizontal stripes worked in two, three or more colours add zing to plain crochet – the stripes can be strongly contrasting in colour or the effect can be more subtle by using a restricted palette of shades of one colour plus one or more coordinating colours. Single crochet, half double crochet, and double crochet stitches all look good worked in stripes.

Chevron stripes are worked in a similar way to plain horizontal stripes, but here stitches are added and subtracted at regular intervals along each row. This forms a pattern of regular peaks and troughs separated by blocks of stitches and creates zigzag patterns. The pattern is set on row 1, then row 2 is repeated until the work is the required length.

JOINING A NEW YARN

Join the new colour at the end of the last row worked in the previous colour. Leaving the last stage of the final stitch incomplete, loop the new yarn round the hook and pull it through the stitches on the hook to complete the stitch, then turn and work the next row with the new colour. You may find it helpful to knot the two loose ends together temporarily before you cut the yarn no longer in use, leaving an end of about 10 cm (4 in.).

WEAVING IN YARN ENDS ON A STRIPE PATTERN

You learned how to deal with yarn ends on page 25, but you need to pay special attention when weaving them in when using more than one yarn colour. Undo the knot securing the two colours, thread the needle with one colour, and weave the end into the wrong side of the same colour of stripe.

STRIPES PATTERN LIBRARY

DOUBLE CROCHET STRIPES

Worked in rows of double crochet stitches, the narrow stripes are of identical widths and arranged in a repeating pattern. Work two rows in yarn A, two in yarn B, two in yarn C, and two in yarn D, then repeat the colour sequence.

TREBLE CROCHET STRIPES

Worked in rows of double crochet stitches, the wide stripes are of identical widths and arranged in a repeating pattern. Work two rows in yarn A, two in yarn B, two in yarn C, and two in yarn D, then repeat the colour sequence. This type of arrangement is also known as a sequenced stripe pattern.

HALF TREBLE CROCHET STRIPES

Worked in rows of half treble crochet stitches, the stripes are of different widths and arranged in a totally random colour sequence. Work several rows in yarn A, then continue working in the same stitch, changing colours at random after one, two, three or more rows have been worked.

CHEVRON STRIPES
Working a basic chevron pattern

STEP 1 To keep the peaks and troughs of chevron stripe patterns correctly spaced, you will need to work one or more extra stitches at the beginning or end (or both) of every row. In this pattern, two double crochet stitches are worked into the first stitch of every row.

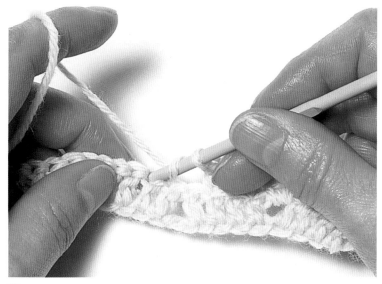

STEP 2
To make the bottom "V" shapes of the chevrons (the troughs), miss two double crochet stitches (miss 2 dc) at the bottom of the troughs, then continue working the next block of stitches.

WORKING AN EYELET CHEVRON PATTERN

STEP 1
In this pattern, the bottom "V" shapes of the chevrons are worked in a similar way to the basic chevron pattern, but because the stitches are longer, small holes (eyelets) are also made. Miss two double crochet stitches (miss 2 sts) at the bottom of the troughs.

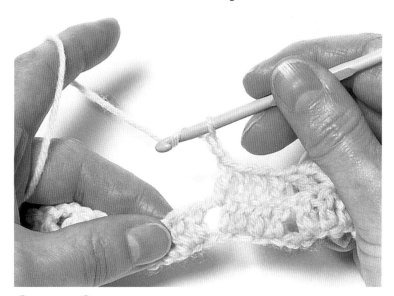

STEP 3
To make the top "V" shapes of the chevrons (the peaks), work three double crochet stitches into the same stitch (3 dc into next dc) at the top of the peaks.

STEP 2
Two chains are worked at the top of each "V" shape to form eyelets. Work the block of stitches before the peak, then work one treble crochet stitch into the eyelet below and work two chains.

STEP 3

To finish the eyelet, work another treble crochet stitch into the eyelet below ([1 dc, 2 ch, 1 dc] into 2 ch sp), then continue working the next block of stitches.

Vary the depth of the stripes and the colour arrangement to give a totally new look to the basic chevron stripes pattern.

BASIC CHEVRON STRIPES

The foundation chain for this pattern requires a multiple of 16 stitches plus 2.

Using yarn A, make the required length of foundation chain.

Row 1 (right side) Work 2 dc into 2nd ch from hook, * 1 dc into each of next 7 ch, miss 1 ch, 1 dc into each of next 7 ch, 3 dc into next ch; rep from * to end omitting 1 dc at end of last rep, turn.

Row 2 1 ch, work 2 dc into first dc, * 1 dc into each of next 7 dc, miss 2 dc, 1 dc into each of next 7 dc, 3 dc into next dc; rep from * to end omitting 1 dc at end of last rep, turn.

Rep row 2, changing yarn colours after every two rows.

EYELET CHEVRON STRIPES

The foundation chain for this pattern requires a multiple of 10 stitches plus 2.

Using yarn A, make the required length of foundation chain.

Row 1 (right side) Miss 2 ch (counts as 1 tr), 1 tr into each of next 4 ch, * miss 2 ch, 1 tr into each of next 4 ch, 2 ch, 1 tr into each of next 4 ch; rep from * to last 6 ch, miss 2 ch, 1 tr into each of next 3 ch, 2 tr into last ch, turn.

Row 2 Ch 3 (counts as 1 tr), 1 tr into first st, 1 tr into each of next 3 sts, * miss 2 sts, 1 tr into each of next 3 sts, [1 tr, 2 ch, 1 tr] into 2 ch sp, 1 tr into each of next 3 sts; rep from * to last 6 sts, miss 2 sts, 1 tr into each of next 3 sts, 2 tr into top of turning ch, turn.

Rep row 2, changing yarn colours after every two rows.

PROJECT 1

CHEVRON STRIPED SCARF

Warm and comfortable to wear in chilly weather, this long scarf is worked in a delightful pattern of chevron stripes using a shaded palette of four neutral colours.

SIZE
25 cm (10 in.) wide, 165 cm (65 in.) long

MATERIALS
QUANTITY 2 x 50 g balls of each colour

YARN "Legend DK" by Sirdar (or any wool and synthetic blend double knitting weight yarn with approx 120 m/131 yd per 50 g ball)

COLOUR 626 Light Grey (A), 628 Taupe (B), 653 Naturelle (C), 621 Cream (D)

HOOK SIZE 3.5 mm, 4 mm (E, F)

NEEDLE Large tapestry needle

SPECIAL TECHNIQUES USED
Working a foundation chain (page 16)
Turning chains (page 18)
Working chevron patterns (page 29–31)
Finishing yarn ends (page 24)

CHECK YOUR TENSION
Make a foundation chain of 39 ch and work approximately 15 cm (6 in.) in pattern, beginning with the foundation row. Block the sample (page 34), allow to dry, and measure the tension (page 44). The recommended tension is 8 rows and 2 pattern repeats to 10 cm (4 in.).

If you have more rows or a smaller pattern repeat, your tension is too tight and you should make another sample using a larger hook.

If you have less rows and a larger pattern repeat, your tension is too loose and you should make another sample using a smaller hook.

ABBREVIATIONS
ch—chain; **tr**—treble crochet; **sl st**—slipstitch; **rep**—repeat

TIP
When making a striped scarf, it's less daunting to deal with the yarn ends as you go instead of leaving them all to do at the end. Weave in the yarn ends on the wrong side of the scarf after every colour change.

NOTES
1. Always read all the way through the pattern before you begin and make sure that you understand the techniques involved.
2. When working a repeating stripe pattern, check after every stripe to make sure that the colour sequence is correct.

Scarf

Using yarn A and the 4 mm (F) hook, work a
loose foundation chain of 52 ch. Change to the
3.5 mm (E) hook to work the rest of the scarf.

Foundation row (right side) Using yarn A, work
1 tr into 4th ch from hook, 1 tr into each of next
3 ch, * 3 tr into next ch, 1 tr into each of next
5 ch, miss 2 ch, 1 tr into each of next 5 ch, rep
from * twice more, 3 tr into next ch, 1 tr into
each of next 5 tr, turn.

Rows 1 and 2 Sl st into 2nd tr, 3 ch (counts as
1 tr), 1 tr into each of next 4 tr, * 3 tr into next
tr, 1 tr into each of next 5 tr, miss 2 tr, 1 tr into
each of next 5 tr, rep from * twice more, 3 tr
into next tr, 1 tr into each of next 5 tr, turn.

Colour sequence

Stripe 1 Break off yarn A, join in yarn B and repeat
rows 1 and 2.

Stripe 2 Break off yarn B, join in yarn C and repeat
rows 1 and 2.

Stripe 3 Break off yarn C, join in yarn D and repeat
rows 1 and 2.

Stripe 4 Break off yarn D, join in yarn A and repeat
rows 1 and 2.

Repeat the two-row stripes in this colour sequence
until the scarf measures approx 165 cm (65 in.),
ending with the 2nd row of stripe 4.
Fasten off yarn.

Finishing

Weave in the yarn ends (see Tip opposite). Press
the scarf very lightly on the wrong side over a
well-padded surface.

ALTERNATIVE SWATCH
*Chevron patterns make strong, colourful
statements when they are worked in stripes, but
can look equally effective worked in a solid
colour or in wide blocks of colour between 8 and
10 rows deep.*

FINISHING

BLOCKING

The first stage of finishing – blocking – involves easing and pinning the crocheted pieces into the correct shape, then either steaming with an iron or moistening with cold water depending on the fibre content of your yarn. Always be guided by the information given on the ball band of your yarn (*see pages 10–11 for details of different yarns and fibres*) and, when in doubt, choose the cold-water blocking method (*see page 35*).

Yarns made from most natural fibres (cotton, linen, wool, but not silk, which is more delicate) can be blocked with warm steam. A large item such as an afghan made in one piece (or from motifs which have been joined together as you go) can be carefully pressed from the wrong side over a well-padded ironing board, using a light touch to avoid crushing the stitches. Never, ever, attempt to steam or press a crochet piece made from man-made yarns such as nylon or acrylic – you will probably melt the yarn, or at the very least flatten it and make it limp and lifeless. Instead, use the cold-water blocking method shown here.

To block garment pieces and separate motifs, it's a good idea to make your own blocking board. You can do this inexpensively by covering a 60 x 90 cm (24 x 36 in.) piece of flat board (a lightweight pinboard made from cork is ideal) with one or two layers of quilter's wadding. Secure the wadding on the back of the board with staples or drawing pins, then cover with a layer of fabric and secure in the same way. Choose fabric made from cotton so it can withstand the heat of the iron – a check pattern is useful so the lines can help you pin out straight edges. Use plenty of rustproof glass-headed pins to pin out the pieces – make sure the pins have glass rather than plastic heads as the latter will melt when heat is applied. When pinning out long pieces such as edgings or borders, work in sections and allow each section to dry completely before moving on to the next one.

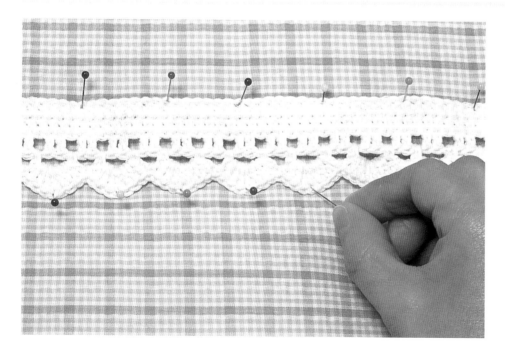

STEP 1 Pin out the crochet piece, using the checks on the fabric to help you keep the edges straight and inserting the pins through the fabric and wadding layers. Be generous with the number of pins you use around the edges, and gently ease the crochet into shape before inserting each pin. Unless the piece is heavily textured and needs to be blocked face-up, you can block crochet with either the right or wrong side facing upwards.

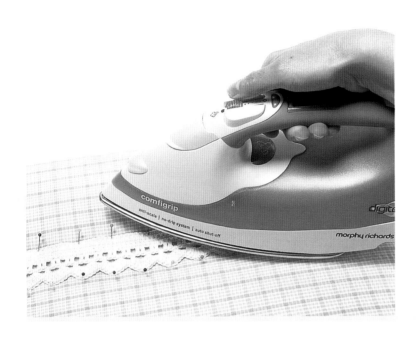

STEP 2

To block natural fibre yarns with warm steam, hold a steam iron set at the correct temperature for the yarn about 2 cm (¾ in.) above the surface of the crochet and allow the steam to penetrate for several seconds. Work in sections and don't allow the iron to come into contact with the crochet surface. Lay the board flat and allow the crochet to dry before removing the pins.

BLOCKING MAN-MADE FIBRE YARNS

Pin out the pieces as above, then use a spray bottle to mist the crochet with clean cold water until it is evenly moist all over, but not saturated. When blocking heavyweight yarns, gently pat the crochet with your hand to help the moisture penetrate more easily. Lay the board flat and allow the crochet to dry before removing the pins.

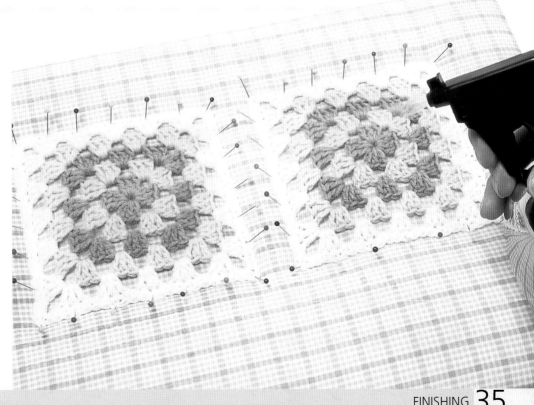

SEAMS

The two methods of joining pieces of crochet shown below are both sewn and are good for finishing garments. Use the same yarn for both crochet fabric and seams, unless your yarn is thick or textured, in which case use a finer yarn of matching colour. A back stitch seam is durable but rather bulky for lightweight garments, so use this method for seaming loose-fitting garments such as winter sweaters. A woven seam gives a flatter finish as the pieces are joined edge to edge. This method works better when finishing fine work and baby garments. Other methods of joining crochet are given on pages 61–63.

BACK STITCH SEAM

Place the pieces to be joined together with the right sides facing and pin, inserting the pins at right angles to the edge. Thread a large tapestry needle with yarn and work a row of back stitch from right to left, close to the edge.

WOVEN SEAM

Place the pieces to be joined side by side on a flat surface with the wrong side facing upwards and the edges touching. Thread a large tapestry needle with yarn and work a row of evenly spaced stitches in a loose zigzag pattern from edge to edge, carefully tightening the tension of the stitches as you work so the edges pull together.

FINISHING EDGES

An edge finish differs from a crochet edging or border (pages 108–111) in the method of working. An edge finish is worked directly into the crochet fabric, unlike an edging or border which is worked separately, then stitched on to crochet or woven fabric as a decoration.

Double crochet edging is used mainly for finishing necklines and borders on garments and it can be worked in a contrasting colour of yarn. Crab stitch edging is more hard-wearing due to the small knots of yarn made along the row. It can be worked directly into the edge of a piece of crochet fabric, as shown, or several rows of double crochet can be worked first to act as a foundation. Picot and shell edgings offer a more decorative finish.

WORKING A DOUBLE CROCHET EDGING

Double crochet is a useful and flexible edge finish. Working from right to left, make a row of ordinary double crochet stitches (pages 19–20) into the edge of the crochet fabric, spacing the stitches evenly along the edge.

WORKING A CRAB STITCH EDGING

STEP 1 Also known as reverse double crochet, this stitch makes a strong, fairly rigid edging with an attractive texture. Unlike most other crochet techniques, this stitch is worked from left to right along the row. Keeping the yarn to the left, insert the hook from front to back into the next stitch and wind the yarn over the hook.

STEP 2
Draw the loop through from back to front so there are now two loops on the hook.

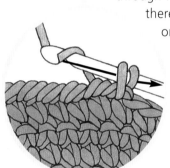

STEP 3
Yarn over hook, then draw the yarn through both loops to complete the stitch.

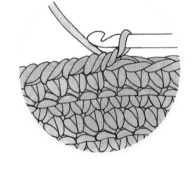

WORKING A PICOT EDGE

STEP 1
This stitch makes a delicate edge with tiny protruding loops of yarn. Work a foundation row of double crochet and turn. * Work 3 ch, slipstitch into 3rd chain from hook (one picot made).

STEP 2 Miss 1 stitch, then work a slipstitch into the next stitch. Repeat from * along the edge.

WORKING A SHELL EDGING

STEP 1 This stitch makes a pretty, wavy edging. Work a foundation row of double crochet, work 1 ch and turn. Work 1 dc into the first stitch, * miss 2 sts, work 5 tr into the next stitch to make a shell.

STEP 2 Miss 2 sts, work 1 dc into the next stitch. Repeat from * along the edge.

BUTTONHOLES AND BUTTON LOOPS

Bands with buttons, buttonholes and loops are best worked in double crochet for strength and neatness. Button loops are a decorative alternative to the ordinary buttonhole, especially for lacy garments. Make the button band first. Mark the positions of the buttons with safety pins and work the buttonhole (or button loop) band to match, making holes or loops opposite the safety pin markers.

STEP 2
Work additional rows of double crochet until the band is the required width for positioning the buttonholes, usually half the total width. Work in double crochet to the position of the buttonhole, miss a few stitches to accommodate the size of the button, and work the same number of chains over the missed stitches. Continue in the same way until all the holes have been worked.

WORKING BUTTONHOLES

STEP 1
Work a row of evenly spaced double crochet (pages 19–20) along the garment edge, with the right side of the garment facing you.

STEP 3
On the next row, work a double crochet into each stitch and each chain along the row.

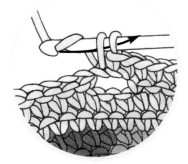

STEP 4
Work additional rows of double crochet until the buttonhole band is the same width as the button band.

WORKING BUTTON LOOPS

STEP 1
Work several rows of double crochet as above until the band is the required width. Work in double crochet to the position of the loop, miss two or three stitches and work a loop of chains to accommodate the button. Continue in the same way until all the loops have been worked.

STEP 2
On the next row, reinforce the loops by working a slipstitch into each stitch and each chain along the row.

PROJECT 2 BUTTONED CUSHIONS

Tweed yarn and decorative buttons make these simple cushion covers into a stylish addition to any room. The buttons can be as fancy as you like and can match or contrast with the yarn colours.

SIZES

Square cushion cover: to fit a 30 cm (12 in.) square cushion pad
Rectangular cushion cover: to fit a 30 x 40 cm (12 x 16 in.) cushion pad

MATERIALS

QUANTITY 3 x 50 g hanks of A, 4 x 50 g hanks of B
YARN "Summer Tweed" by Rowan (or novelty Aran weight yarn with approx 108 m/118 yd per 50 g hank)
COLOUR 500 Powder (A), 511 Cape (B)
HOOK SIZE 4 mm, 4.5 mm (F, G)
NEEDLE Large tapestry needle
Finer smooth yarn in matching colours for sewing up
Decorative buttons

SPECIAL TECHNIQUES USED

Working a foundation chain (page 16)
Turning chains (page 25)
Working into the back and front of the stitch (page 24)
Working buttonholes (page 40)

CHECK YOUR TENSION

Using the 4 mm (F) hook, make a foundation chain of 36 ch and work approximately 15 cm (6 in.) in pattern. Block and press the sample, allow to dry, and measure the tension (page 44). The recommended tension is 18 stitches and 7 rows to 10 cm (4 in.).

If you have more stitches and rows, your tension is too tight and you should make another sample using a larger hook.

If you have less stitches and rows, your tension is too loose and you should make another sample using a smaller hook.

ABBREVIATIONS

ch—chain; **dc**—double crochet; **tr**—treble crochet; **sl st**—slipstitch; **rep**—repeat, **WS**—wrong side; **incl**—including

TIP

Tension is fairly tight when making this project – this makes a stiffer, stronger fabric which will wear well and won't stretch out of shape. If you find a tight tension makes it difficult for you to work the stitches easily, change to a size larger hook. More information about tension is given on page 44.

NOTES

1. Always read all the way through the pattern before you begin and make sure that you understand the techniques involved.
2. Wind the yarn into balls before you begin.

Square Cushion

Using yarn A and the 4.5 mm (G) hook, work a foundation ch of 57 plus 3 turning ch. Change to the 4 mm (F) hook.

Foundation row (wrong side) Work 1 tr into 4th ch from hook, 1 tr into each ch along row, turn (58 tr, incl turning ch which counts as 1tr).

Row 1 (right side) 3 ch (counts as 1 tr), 1 tr into back loop of each tr along row, 1 tr into 3rd of 3 ch, turn.

Row 2 (wrong side) 3 ch, 1 tr into front loop of each tr along row, 1 tr into 3rd of 3 ch, turn (58 tr, incl turning ch which counts as 1 tr).

Work straight, rep rows 1 and 2 until work measures 63.5 cm (25 in.), ending with a WS row.

Next row (right side) 1 ch, work 1 dc into back loop of each tr along row.

Next row (wrong side) 1 ch, work 1 dc into both loops of each dc along row.

Make buttonholes

Next row Work in dc through both loops, making 4 evenly spaced buttonholes along the row.
Work 3 rows of dc through both loops.
Fasten off yarn.

Rectangular Cushion

Using yarn B and the 4.5 mm (G) hook, work a foundation ch of 75 plus 3 turning ch. Change to the 4 mm (F) hook.

Foundation row (wrong side) Work 1 tr into 4th ch from hook, 1 tr into each ch along row, turn (76 tr, incl turning ch which counts as 1 tr).

Row 1 (right side) 3 ch (counts as 1 dc), 1 dc into back loop of each dc along row, 1 dc into 3rd of 3 ch, turn.

Row 2 (wrong side) 3 ch, 1 tr into front loop of each tr along row, 1 tr into 3rd of 3 ch, turn (76 tr, incl turning ch which counts as 1 tr).

Work straight, rep rows 1 and 2 until work measures 63.5 cm (25 in.), ending with a WS row.

Next row (right side) 1 ch, work 1 dc into back loop of each tr along row.

Next row (wrong side) 1 ch, work 1 dc into both loops of each dc along row.

Make buttonholes

Next row Work in dc through both loops, making 6 evenly spaced buttonholes along the row.
Work 3 rows of dc through both loops.
Fasten off yarn.

To finish both cushions

Weave in the yarn ends, block (page 34) and allow to dry completely.

Fold the buttonhole edge over with RS together to make a 22 cm (8½ in.) deep flap and pin in position. Fold over the opposite end to make a 15 cm (6 in.) deep flap and pin in position. Stitch the seams using backstitch (page 36) and the smooth yarn. Turn to the right side. Sew on the buttons to correspond with the buttonholes and insert cushion pad.

ALTERNATIVE SWATCH
Originally worked in a silk and cotton mix yarn with a tweedy texture, the cushion covers would look equally effective worked in a smooth yarn. Choose an Aran weight yarn and decorate the covers with plain chunky buttons made from wood or marbled plastic.

TENSION

The term "tension" refers to the number of stitches and rows contained in a given width and length of crochet fabric. Crochet patterns include a recommended tension for the yarn which has been used to make the item shown and it's important that you match this tension exactly so your work comes out the right size. This is usually quoted as x stitches and y rows to 10 cm (4 in.) measured over a certain stitch pattern using a certain size of hook. The information may vary to include a measurement taken across one or more pattern repeats. Working to the suggested tension will also make sure that the crochet fabric is neither too heavy and stiff, nor loose and floppy in use. Yarn ball bands may also quote a recommended tension as well as giving information on fibre composition, yardage and care.

Tension can be affected by the type of yarn used, the size and brand of the crochet hook, the type of stitch pattern and the tension of an individual worker. Crochet fabric has less "give" and elasticity than a comparable knitted fabric so it's crucial to test the tension before you begin making any item, particularly a garment. As a general rule, accessories (handbags, hats) and home furnishings (cushion covers, lace edgings) are worked to a tighter tension than scarves, garments, and afghans, which need a softer type of fabric.

YARN VARIATIONS

Always try to use the exact yarn quoted in the pattern instructions. Two yarns with the same description (e.g. 4ply or Aran) and fibre content made by different manufacturers will vary slightly in thickness. The colour of yarn you choose may also affect tension as a result of the different dyes used in manufacture.

HOOK VARIATIONS

Hooks from different manufacturers and those made from different materials can vary widely in shape and size even though they may all be branded with the same number or letter. The size of a hand-carved wooden hook will vary from that of a machine-made resin or aluminium hook. You'll probably find that you prefer the feel of one type of hook so it's a good idea to buy several consecutive sizes once you've made your choice. Always use the same hook for working both the tension sample and the finished item. You can find more information about crochet hooks on page 12.

STITCH PATTERNS

Some stitch patterns have the effect of reducing or expanding the crochet widthways, and others have the same effect lengthways. These differences are particularly crucial when working a garment, so always work the tension sample in the exact pattern you will use for the main piece.

SUBSTITUTING YARNS

When you cannot obtain the exact yarn used in the pattern, you will probably be able to find one that is similar. Read the pattern instructions and make a note of the recommended tension, hook size, fibre content and yardage, if quoted. Try to find a substitute yarn that matches all these criteria as closely as possible, paying particular attention to the tension. Buy one ball of the yarn and experiment with making tension samples until your sample matches the tension in the pattern (see below).

When purchasing the bulk of the yarn, don't forget that if the substitute yarn has a shorter yardage (quoted on the ball band of many yarns) than the original, you will need to purchase extra yarn. As a general rule, man-made yarns are lighter and have a longer yardage than woollen yarns. Cotton and cotton-blend yarns are usually heavy and will have a shorter yardage than man-made or woollen yarns. When in doubt, it's a good idea to buy an extra ball of yarn instead of running out at a crucial moment.

HOW TO ADJUST THE TENSION

If you have more stitches or a smaller pattern repeat between the pins inserted in your tension sample, your tension is too tight and you should make another sample using a hook one size larger.

If you have less stitches and a larger pattern repeat between the pins inserted in your tension sample, your tension is too loose and you should make another sample using a hook one size smaller.

Block the new sample as before and measure the tension as above. Repeat this process until your tension matches that given in the pattern.

MAKING AND MEASURING A TENSION SAMPLE

Read the pattern instructions to find the recommended tension. Working in the exact yarn you will use for the item, make a generously sized sample 15–20 cm (6–8 in.) wide. If you are working a stitch pattern, choose a number of foundation chains to suit the stitch repeat. Work in the required pattern until the piece is 15–20 cm (6–8 in.) long. Fasten off the yarn. Block the tension sample using the method suited to the yarn composition (pages 34–35) and allow to dry.

STEP 1 Lay the sample right side up on a flat surface and use a ruler or tape measure to measure 10 cm (4 in.) horizontally across a row of stitches. Mark this measurement by inserting two pins exactly 10 cm (4 in.) apart. Make a note of the number of stitches (including partial stitches) between the pins. This is the number of stitches to 10 cm (4 in.).

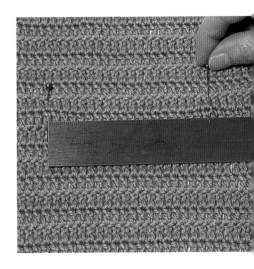

STEP 2 Turn the sample on its side. Working in the same way, measure 10 cm (4 in.) across the rows, again inserting two pins exactly 10 cm (4 in.) apart. Make a note of the number of rows (including partial rows) between the pins. This is the number of rows to 10 cm (4 in.).

STEP 3 When working a particular stitch pattern, tension information may be quoted as a multiple of the pattern repeat, rather than as a set number of rows and stitches. Work your tension sample in pattern, but this time count repeats instead of rows and stitches between the pins.

UNDERSTANDING PATTERNS

In addition to the standard abbreviations given below, there may be special abbreviations for the particular pattern you are working. These will be explained on the relevant pattern.

STANDARD CROCHET ABBREVIATIONS

ch(s)—chain(s)
sl st—slipstitch
dc—double crochet
htr—half treble crochet
tr—treble crochet
dtr—double treble crochet
st(s)—stitch(es)
sp(s)— space(s)
lp(s)—loop(s)
rep—repeat
yoh—yarn over hook
rem—remaining
cont—continue
alt—alternate
beg—beginning
foll—following
patt—pattern

FOLLOWING A PATTERN

Crochet pattern instructions are laid out in a logical sequence, although at first sight the terminology can look rather complicated. The most important thing to remember when following a pattern is to check that you start off with the correct number of stitches in the foundation row or ring, and then work through the instructions row-by-row exactly as stated.

WHAT DO BRACKETS, ASTERISKS, DAGGERS, AND STARS INDICATE?

Brackets, asterisks, daggers, and stars are used in order to make written patterns shorter and avoid tedious repetition. The instructions will be phrased slightly differently depending on whether square brackets or symbols are used, and both may be used together in the same pattern row of a complex design.

BRACKETS

The sequence of stitches enclosed inside brackets [] must be worked as instructed. For example, [1 tr into the next 3 sts, 2 ch] 4 times means that you will work the three treble crochet stitches and the two chains four times in all. The same number of stitches is worked as in the asterisked example below, but here the same information is stated in a slightly different way.

PARENTHESES

Parentheses () contain extra information, not instructions to be worked. For example, Row 1 (right side) means that the right side of the work is facing you as you work this row. Parentheses are also used to indicate the number of different sizes in which a garment pattern is worked, as well as the different numbers of stitches. In this case, it's often helpful to read all the way through the pattern and highlight the corresponding numbers as an aid to easy reading. You may also find a number enclosed in parentheses at the end of a row or round – this indicates the total number of stitches to work in that particular row or round. For example, (12 spaced tr) at the end of a round means that you have to work 12 treble crochet stitches in the round, each one spaced out by the number of chains stated in the instructions.

ASTERISKS *, DAGGERS †, AND STARS ☆

Asterisks are the most widely used symbol in crochet instructions, but the other two may appear in complex patterns. Any of the symbols may be used to indicate that you must repeat the sequence of stitches (or the instructions) that follow the symbol. You must repeat the sequence in addition to the first time you work it. For example, * 1 tr into each of the next 3 sts, 2 ch; rep from * 3 times means you need to work the three treble crochet stitches and the two chains four times in all. These symbols fulfil a similar function to brackets.

You may also find asterisks used in instructions that tell you how to work any stitches remaining after the last complete repeat of a stitch sequence is worked. For example, rep from * to end, ending with 1 dc into each of last 2 sts, turn means that you have two stitches left at the end of the row after working the last repeat. In this case, work one double crochet stitch into each of the last two stitches before turning to begin next row.

REPEATS

Each stitch pattern, worked in rows, is written using a specific number of pattern rows and the sequence is repeated until the crochet is the correct length. When working a complicated stitch pattern, always make a note of exactly which row you are working. Write the row number in a notebook, or on a piece of paper with a pencil (you may find that a knitter's row counter is useful), as it's very easy to forget exactly which row you

are working on when your crochet session gets interrupted. Avoid using a fibre-tipped or ball point pen when making notes as ink can easily get on your fingers and may be transferred to the yarn you are using.

CHARTED PATTERNS

With the exception of filet crochet patterns, which are always worked from a chart (page 82), most crochet patterns found across the English-speaking world use written instructions to describe the method of working. The majority of crochet patterns originating from Europe (with the exception of Britain) are charts using symbols to indicate the different stitches and how they are placed. The symbols have been standardized so that the same ones can be used throughout the world. A charted pattern still contains some written instructions, but the stitch patterns are shown in a visual form. Charted instructions also solve the problem of translating lengthy written instructions from one language to another.

To use a charted pattern, first familiarize yourself with the different symbols and their meanings. These are explained in a key at the side of the chart. Each symbol represents a single instruction or stitch, and indicates exactly where to work the

stitch. Follow the numerical sequence on the chart whether you are working in rows or rounds. In the same way as using a written pattern, keep a note of which row or round you are working to avoid confusion.

The chart below shows the main symbols used in crochet charts, with both United Kingdom and United States terminology.

THE BASIC INTERNATIONAL CROCHET SYMBOLS

UK		USA
start here	▲	start here
fasten off	△	fasten off
chain	⬯	chain
slipstitch	⬬	slip stitch
double crochet	+	single crochet
half treble crochet	┬	half double crochet
treble crochet	✗	double crochet
double treble	✗	treble (triple)
treble crochet through back loop only	✗	double crochet through back loop only
treble crochet through front loop only	✗	double crochet through front loop only
repeat (between two of these)	✳	repeat (between two of these)

PROJECT 3 CHILD'S SWEATER

This generously proportioned child's T-shaped sweater is available in a wide range of sizes. Quick to work in plain treble crochet stitches, the sweater is trimmed at hem, neck and cuffs with narrow bands of contrasting colour.

SIZES

TO FIT BUST/CHEST	61 [66, 71, 76, 81] cm (24 [26, 28, 30, 32] in.)
ACTUAL MEASUREMENT	68.5 [73.5, 79, 84, 89] cm (27 [29, 31, 33, 35] in.)
SIDE LENGTH	22 [24, 26, 28, 30] cm (8¾ [9½, 10¼, 11, 11¾] in.)
SLEEVE LENGTH (measured straight from top of sleeve to cuff edge)	28 [30.5, 33, 35.5, 38] cm (11 [12, 13, 14, 15] in.)

MATERIALS

QUANTITY 5 [5, 6, 6, 7] x 50 g balls of A, 1 [1, 1, 1, 1] ball of B

YARN "Rio" Cotton Rich Double Knitting by Sirdar (or 60% cotton and 40% acrylic DK yarn with approx 132 m/144 yd per 50 g ball)

COLOUR 052 Buttercup (A), 051 Lime (B)

HOOK SIZE 3.5 mm, 4 mm (Size E, F)

NEEDLE Large tapestry needle

SPECIAL TECHNIQUES USED

Making a foundation chain (page 17)
Turning chains (page 18)
Increasing (pages 50–51)
Working a double crochet edging (page 37)

CHECK YOUR TENSION

Make a foundation chain of 24 ch using the 4 mm (F) hook and work approximately 15 cm (6 in.) in treble crochet. Block the sample (page 35), allow to dry, and measure the tension (page 44). The recommended tension is 16 stitches and 9 rows to 10 cm (4 in.).

If you have more stitches and rows, your tension is too tight and you should make another sample using a larger hook.

If you have less stitches and rows, your tension is too loose and you should make another sample using a smaller hook.

ABBREVIATIONS

ch—chain; **tr**—treble crochet; **inc**—increase

TIP

When working with a yarn containing a high percentage of cotton, you may find that the yarn has very little "give". If you find that the foundation chains are too tight to insert the hook comfortably when working the first row of stitches, redo the chain using a size larger hook.

NOTES

1. Always read all the way through the pattern before you begin and make sure that you understand the techniques involved.
2. Figures in square brackets [ ] refer to the larger sizes. Where only one figure is given it refers to all sizes.

(36 [38, 40, 42, 44] tr incl turning ch which
counts as 1 tr).

Row 1 3 ch, work 1 tr into each tr along row,
1 tr into 3rd of 3 ch, turn.

Rep row 1, at the same time inc 1 st at the beg
and end of every 4th row 5 [5, 6, 6, 7] times in
all. (46 [48, 52, 54, 58] tr, incl turning ch which
counts as 1 tr).

Work straight until sleeve measures 28 [30.5, 33,
35.5, 38] cm (11 [12, 13, 14, 15] in.).

Fasten off yarn.

FINISHING

Weave in the short yarn ends, block each piece and
allow to dry completely.

With right sides together, join the front and back
together at the shoulders, leaving the centre 15
[16.5, 18, 19, 20] cm (6 [6½, 7, 7½, 8] in.) open,
using one of the methods on page 36.

Measure the top of the sleeves and mark the centre
point with a pin. With right sides together, join
the sleeves to the front and back aligning the
centre points with the shoulder seams.

With right sides together, join the sleeve and side
seams.

WORKING THE EDGING

Using yarn B and the 3.5 mm (E) hook, work one
row of double crochet edging (page 37) around
the neck, cuffs, and lower edge of the sweater,
fastening off the yarn ends neatly.

BACK

Using yarn A and the F (4 mm) hook, 53 ch
[57, 61, 65, 70] plus 3 turning ch.

Foundation row (right side) Insert hook into 4th
ch from hook, work 1 tr in each ch to end, turn.
(54 [58, 62, 66, 71] tr incl turning ch which
counts as 1 tr).

Row 1 3 ch, work 1 tr into each tr along row,
1 tr into 3rd of 3 ch, turn.

Work straight, repeating row 1, until the work
measures 35 [37, 39, 41, 43] cm (13¾ [14½, 15¼,
16, 17] in.).

Fasten off yarn.

FRONT

Work the same as for the back.

SLEEVES (MAKE 2)

Using yarn A and the 4 mm (F) hook, 35 [37, 39,
41, 43] ch plus 3 turning ch.

Foundation row (right side) Insert hook into 4th
ch from hook, work 1 tr in each ch to end, turn.

ALTERNATIVE SWATCH

*To liven up a kid's plain sweater, make a small
circular motif by joining six chains into a ring, then
working one round of treble crochet stitches into
the ring (pages 56–58). Repeat
several times using one or
more contrasting colours,
then stitch the motifs
randomly onto the front
of the sweater using
matching thread.*

SHAPING

Shaping by adding or subtracting one or two stitches can take place at intervals along a row of crochet – this is known as working internal increases or decreases. When stitches are added or subtracted at the beginning and end of specified rows, this is known as working external increases or decreases.

WORKING AN INTERNAL DOUBLE INCREASE

To work a double increase (to add two stitches) at intervals along the row, simply work three stitches into one stitch on the previous row.

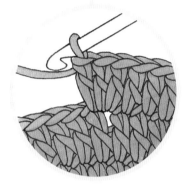

WORKING AN INTERNAL SINGLE INCREASE

The simplest method of adding a single stitch at intervals along a row of crochet is by working two stitches into one stitch on the previous row.

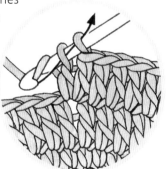

MAKING A NEAT EDGE WHEN SHAPING

STEP 1 Single and double increases are often used at the beginning and end of rows to shape garment edges. To do this neatly at the start of a row, work the first stitch and then work the increase.

STEP 2 At the end of the row, work until two stitches remain (the last stitch will probably be the turning chain from the previous row). Work the increase into the penultimate stitch, then work the last stitch as usual.

WORKING AN EXTERNAL INCREASE

STEP 1 To increase several stitches at one time, you will need to add extra foundation chains at the appropriate end of the row. To add stitches at the beginning of a row, work the required number of extra chains at the end of the previous row. Don't forget to add the correct number of turning chains (page 18) for the stitch you are using.

STEP 2 Turn and work back along the extra chains, then work the row in the usual way.

WORKING AN INTERNAL DECREASE BY SKIPPING A STITCH

STEP 3 To add stitches at the end of
a row, leave the last few stitches of the row
unworked. Remove the hook. Join a length
of yarn to the last stitch of the row and
work the required number of extra chains,
then fasten off the yarn.

The simplest method of removing a single stitch at
intervals along a row of crochet is by missing one stitch
of the previous row.

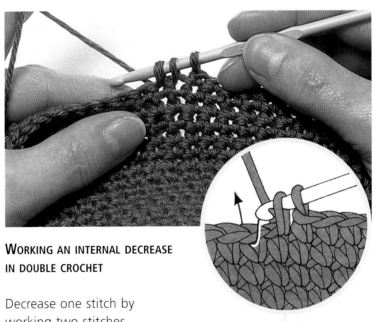

**WORKING AN INTERNAL DECREASE
IN DOUBLE CROCHET**

STEP 4 Insert the hook back into
the row and continue, working extra
stitches across the chains. Turn and work
the next row in the usual way.

Decrease one stitch by
working two stitches
together (dc2tog). Leave the
first stitch incomplete (two
loops on the hook), draw the
yarn through the next stitch
(three loops on the hook).
Yarn over and pull through
all three loops to finish.
Decrease two stitches by
working three stitches
together (dc3tog).

Working an internal decrease in treble crochet

Decrease one treble crochet stitch by working two stitches together (known as tr2tog). Leave the first stitch incomplete so there are two loops on the hook, then work another incomplete stitch so you have three loops on the hook. Yarn over and pull through all three loops to finish the decrease. Two stitches can be decreased in the same way by working three treble crochet stitches together (tr3tog).

To make a neat edge when shaping a garment, work the decrease one stitch in from the edge in the same way as a single or double increase (pages 50–51).

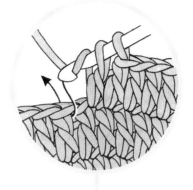

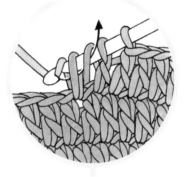

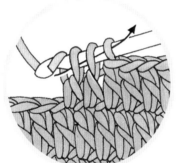

Working an external decrease

STEP 1 To decrease several stitches at one time at the beginning of a row, turn, work a slip stitch into each of the stitches to be decreased, then work the appropriate turning chain and continue along the row.

STEP 2 At the end of the row, simply leave the stitches to be decreased unworked, work the appropriate turning chain, turn, and continue along the row.

NECK BAG AND SHOULDER BAG

Make this stylish duo of neck and shoulder bag from sparkly metallic yarn to wear in the evenings, or from sturdy cotton yarn for everyday use.

SIZES

Neck bag: 10 cm (4 in.) square
Bag with shoulder strap: 15 cm (6 in.) wide, 19 cm (7½ in.) long

MATERIALS

QUANTITY 2 x 25 g balls of A, 4 x 25 g balls of B
YARN "Lurex Shimmer" by Rowan (or viscose/polyester metallic yarn with approx 95 m per/104 yd 25 g ball)
COLOUR 333 Pewter (A), 337 Minty (B)
HOOK SIZE 3 mm, 3.5 mm (C, E)
NEEDLE Large tapestry needle
Small and large decorative buttons with shanks

SPECIAL TECHNIQUES USED

Working a foundation chain (page 16)
Turning chains (page 18)
Shaping (page 50)
Making cords (page 118-119)

CHECK YOUR TENSION

Using yarn A double and the 3.5 mm (E) hook, make a foundation chain of 33 ch and work approximately 15 cm (6 in.) in dc. Block (page 34) the sample, allow to dry, and measure the tension (page 44). The recommended tension for yarn A is 22 stitches and 24 rows to 10 cm (4 in.).

Using yarn B double and the E (3.5 mm) hook, make a foundation chain of 30 ch and work approximately 6 in. (15 cm) in htr. Block (page 34) the sample, allow to dry, and measure the tension (page 44). The recommended tension for yarn B is 20 stitches and 15 rows to 4 in. (10 cm).

If you have more stitches and rows, your tension is too tight and you should make another sample using a larger hook.

If you have less stitches and rows, your tension is too loose and you should make another sample using a smaller hook.

ABBREVIATIONS

ch—chain; **dc**—double crochet; **htr**—half treble crochet; **sl st**—slipstitch; **st(s)**—stitch(es); **beg**—beginning; **RS**—right side; **WS**—wrong side; **incl**—including

TIP

Tension is fairly tight when making this project – this makes a stiffer, stronger fabric which will wear well and won't stretch out of shape. If you find a tight tension makes it difficult for you to work the stitches easily, change to a size larger hook. More information about tension is given on page 44.

NOTES

1. Always read all the way through the pattern before you begin and make sure that you understand the techniques involved.
2. The yarn is used double throughout.

Neck Bag

Using yarn A double and the 3.5 mm (E) hook, work a foundation ch of 20 plus 1 turning ch.

Row 1 (right side) Work 1 dc into 2nd ch from hook, 1 dc into each ch along row, turn (20 dc).

Row 2 1 ch, work 1 dc each dc along row, turn.

Repeat row 2 until work measures 20 cm (8 in.) from beg, ending with a WS row.

Shape flap

Next row (right side) 1 ch, miss first dc to decrease 1 stitch, work dc along the row, turn (19 dc).

Repeat this row until 2 sts remain.

Fasten off yarn, leaving a long end to make button loop.

Make cord

Using yarn A double and the 3.5 mm (E) hook, make a foundation chain about 5 cm (2 in.) longer than required. Change to the 3 mm (C) hook and work a row of sl st along one side of the chain.

Fasten off yarn.

Bag with Shoulder Strap

Using yarn B double and the 3.5 mm (E) hook, work a foundation ch of 29 plus 2 turning ch.

Row 1 (right side) Work 1 htr into 3rd ch from hook, 1 htr into each ch along row, turn (30 htr, incl turning ch which counts as 1 htr).

Row 2 (wrong side) 2 ch (counts as 1 htr), work 1 htr into each st along row, 1 htr into 2nd of 2 ch, turn (30 htr).

Repeat row 2 until work measures 38 cm (15 in.) from beg, ending with a WS row.

Shape flap

Next row (right side) 2 ch, work 1 htr into first 2 sts, miss 1 st, work htr along the row to last 3 sts, miss 1 st, 1 htr into next st, 1 htr into 2nd of 2 ch, turn (28 htr, incl turning ch which counts as 1 htr).

Repeat this row until 4 sts remain.

Next row 1 ch, work 1 dc into each st. Fasten off yarn, leaving a long end to make button loop.

Make cord

Using yarn B double and the 3.5 mm (E) hook, make a foundation chain about 5 cm (2 in.) longer than required. Change to the 3 mm (C) hook and work a row of sl st along both sides of the chain.

Fasten off yarn.

Finishing

Both bags: Use the yarn end at the point of each flap to crochet a chain long enough to accommodate the button. Secure the end of the chains on the wrong side of the flaps. Weave in the yarn ends, block (page 34). Fold up the first 10 cm (4 in.) [19 cm (7½ in.)] with RS together so the foundation chain is level with the start of the shaping. Stitch the side edges together and turn to the right side. Fold over the flap on to the front of the bags and mark the position of the button loop with a pin. Stitch the buttons and cord ends securely to the purse.

WORKING IN ROUNDS

Working crochet in rounds rather than straight rows offers a new range of possibilities to make colourful and intricate pieces of crochet called "motifs". The motifs are all worked outwards from a central ring and can be circular, square, triangular, hexagonal or octagonal in shape, and solid, textured or lacy in appearance. They are joined together using a variety of techniques to make afghans, shawls and wraps, as well as simply shaped garments.

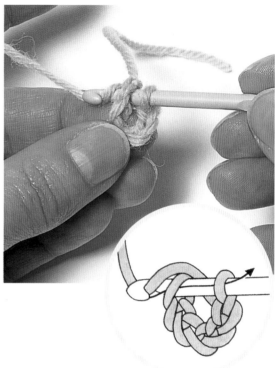

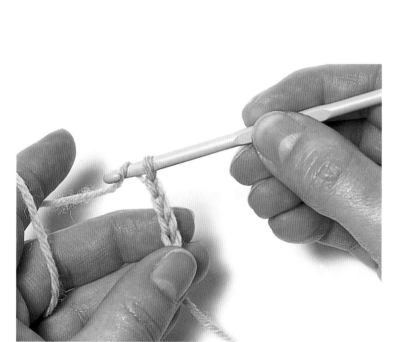

MAKING A RING OF STITCHES

STEP 1 Begin making the foundation ring by working a short length of foundation chain (page 16) as specified in the pattern.

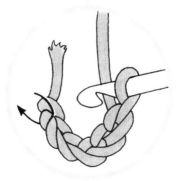

STEP 2 Join the chains into a ring by working a slipstitch into the first stitch of the foundation chain.

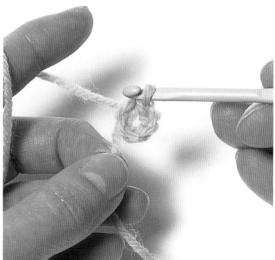

STEP 3 Gently tighten the first stitch by pulling the loose yarn end with your left hand. The foundation ring is now complete.

WORKING INTO THE RING

STEP 1 You are now ready to begin the first round of pattern. Work the number of turning chains specified in the pattern – three chains are shown here and will count as a treble crochet stitch.

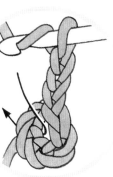

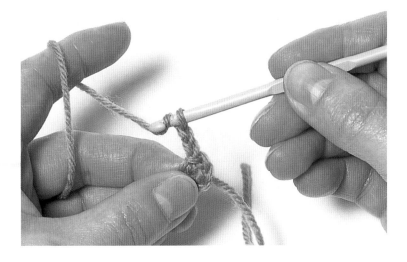

STEP 2 Inserting the hook into the space at the centre of the ring each time, work the correct number of stitches into the ring as specified in the pattern. Count the stitches at the end of the round to make sure you have worked the correct number.

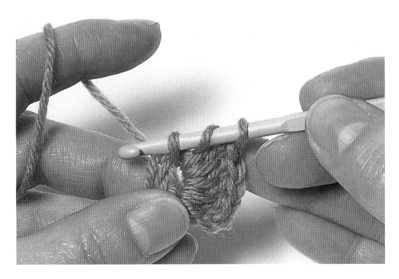

STEP 3 Join the first and last stitches of the round together by working a slipstitch into the top of the turning chain.

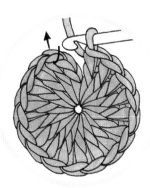

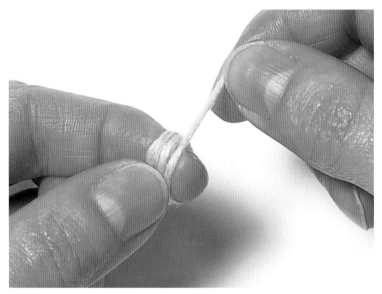

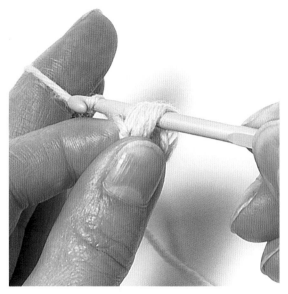

Making a yarn ring

STEP 1 This method of making a foundation ring is useful because the yarn end is enclosed with the first round of stitches and will not need to be woven in later. It should not be used with slippery cotton, man-made or silk yarns, because the yarn ends may eventually work loose. Begin by holding the yarn end between the thumb and first finger of your left hand and wind the yarn several times round the tip of your finger.

STEP 2 Carefully slip the yarn ring off your finger. Inserting the hook into the ring, pull a loop of yarn through and work a double crochet stitch to secure the ring. Work the specified number of turning chains and the first round of pattern into the ring in the usual way.

Finishing off the final round

STEP 1 For a really neat edge, finish off the final round by using this method of sewing the first and last stitches together in preference to the slipstitch method shown on page 57. Cut the yarn, leaving an end of about 10 cm (4 in.) and draw it though the last stitch. With right side facing, thread the end in a large tapestry needle and take it under both loops of the stitch next to the turning chain.

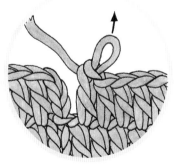

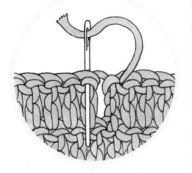

CIRCULAR MOTIFS PATTERN LIBRARY

Circular motifs are often used separately in a variety of yarns and sizes to make items such as coasters and table mats. They join less easily than motifs with straight sides because of their curved shape, and are best sewn together where the curves touch.

STEP 2 Pull the
needle through, insert it into the centre of the last stitch of the round. On the wrong side, pull the needle through to complete the stitch, adjust the length of the stitch to close the round, then weave in the end on the wrong side in the usual way.

STRIPED CIRCLE

This motif can be made larger than shown by working one more treble crochet stitch between the increases on each round.

Foundation ring Using yarn A, 6 ch and join with sl st to form a ring.

Round 1 3 ch (counts as 1 tr), work 15 tr into ring, join with sl st into 3rd of 3 ch. (16 tr). Break off yarn A.

Round 2 Using yarn B, 3 ch (counts as 1 tr), 1 tr in same place, 2 tr into each st of previous round, join with sl st into 3rd of 3 ch. (32 tr). Break off yarn B.

Round 3 Using yarn C, 3 ch (counts as 1 tr), 1 tr in same place, * 1 tr in next st, 2 tr in next st; rep from * to last st, 1 tr in last st, join with sl st into 3rd of 3 ch. (48 tr). Break off yarn C.

Round 4 Using yarn A, 3 ch (counts as 1 tr), 1 tr in same place, * 1 tr into each of next 2 sts, 2 tr into next st; rep from * to last 2 sts, 1 tr into each of last 2 sts, join with sl st into 3rd of 3 ch. (64 tr). Fasten off yarn.

CIRCLE WITH SPOKES

Foundation ring 6 ch and join with sl st to form a ring.

Round 1 5 ch (counts as 1 tr, 2 ch), work 1 tr, 2 ch into ring 7 times, join with sl st into 3rd of 5 ch. (8 spaced tr).

Round 2 3 ch (counts as 1 tr), 2 tr into same tr, 2 ch, [3 tr into next tr, 2 ch] 7 times, join with sl st into 3rd of 3 ch.

Round 3 3 ch (counts as 1 tr), 1 tr into same place, 1 tr into next tr, 2 tr into next tr, 2 ch, [2 tr into next tr, 1 tr into next tr, 2 tr into next tr, 2 ch] 7 times, join with sl st into 3rd of 3 ch.

Round 4 1 ch, work 1 dc into each tr and 2 dc into each 2 ch sp, join with sl st into first dc.
Fasten off yarn.

SQUARE MOTIFS PATTERN LIBRARY

Square motifs are worked in a similar way to circular motifs, but extra stitches or chains are added at regular intervals to form the corners.

HARMONY SQUARE

Foundation ring Using yarn A, 4 ch and join with sl st to form a ring.

Round 1 5 ch (counts as 1 tr, 2 ch), [3 tr into ring, 2 ch] 3 times. 2 tr into ring, join with sl st into 3rd of 5 ch. (four groups of 3 tr, four 2 ch sp(s) forming corners). Break off yarn A.

Round 2 Join yarn B to 2 ch sp. 7 ch (counts as 1 tr, 4 ch), * 2 tr into same 2 ch sp, 1 tr into each tr across side of square, † 2 tr into next 2 ch sp, 4 ch; rep from * twice and from * to † again, 1 tr into same 2 ch sp, join with sl st into 3rd of 7 ch. (four groups of 7 tr, four 4 ch sp(s) forming corners). Break off yarn B.

Round 3 Join yarn C to 4 ch sp. Rep round 2. (four groups of 11 tr, four 4 ch sp(s) forming corners).

Round 4 Rep round 2. (four groups of 15 tr, four 4 ch sp(s) forming corners). Fasten off yarn.

SAINT GEORGE SQUARE

Foundation ring 6 ch and join with sl st to form a ring.

Round 1 3 ch (counts as 1 tr), work 15 tr into ring, join with sl st into 3rd of 3 ch. (16 tr).

Round 2 3 ch (counts as 1 tr), 2 tr into same st as sl st, 2 ch, miss 1 tr, 1 tr into next tr, 2 ch, miss 1 tr, * 3 tr into next tr, 2 ch, miss 1 tr, 1 tr into next tr, 2 ch, miss 1 tr; rep from * twice, join with sl st into 3rd of 3 ch.

Round 3 3 ch (counts as 1 tr), 5 tr into next tr, * 1 tr into next tr, [2 ch, 1 tr into next tr] twice, 5 tr into next tr; rep from * twice, [1 tr into next tr, 2 ch] twice, join with sl st into 3rd of 3 ch.

Round 4 3 ch, 1 tr into each of next 2 tr, 5 tr into next tr, * 1 tr into each of next 3 tr, 2 ch, 1 tr into next tr, 2 ch, 1 tr into each of next 3 tr, 5 tr into next tr; rep from * twice, 1 tr into each of next 3 tr, 2 ch, 1 tr into next tr, 2ch, join with sl st into 3rd of 3 ch.

Round 5 3 ch, 1 tr into each of next 4 tr, [2 tr, 2 ch, 2 tr] into next tr, * 1 tr into each of next 5 tr, 2 tr into next 2 ch sp, 1 tr into next tr, 2 tr into next 2 ch sp, 1 tr into each of next 5 tr, [2 tr, 2 ch, 2 tr] into next dc; rep from * twice, 1 tr into each of next 5 tr, 2 tr into next 2 ch sp, 1 tr into next tr, 2 tr into next 2 ch sp, join with sl st into 3rd of 3 ch.
Fasten off yarn.

JOINING MOTIFS

Motifs can be joined, either by sewing them together, or with rows of slipstitch or double crochet. When using the sewing methods below and on page 62, stitch with yarn to match the last round of crochet. Also, use matching yarn when joining with crochet, but remember that you can make a decorative statement when using slipstitch by choosing a contrasting colour of yarn.

SEWING THROUGH THE BACK LOOPS

STEP 1 Lay out the motifs to be joined in the correct order with the right side of each motif facing upwards. Working first in horizontal rows, overcast the motifs together, beginning with the top row of motifs. Begin stitching at the right-hand edge of the first two motifs, inserting the needle into the back loop of corresponding stitches.

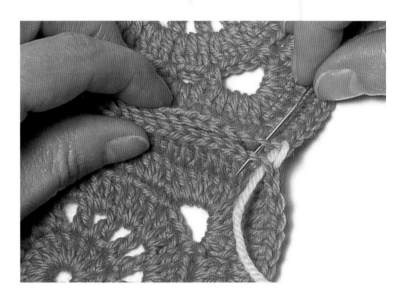

STEP 2 Continue overcasting the first two motifs together, making sure you join only the back loops of each edge together, until you reach the left-hand corner. Align the next two motifs, carry the thread firmly across and join them together in the same way. For extra strength, you can work two stitches into the corner loops before and after carrying the thread across. Continue joining motifs along the row, then secure the thread carefully at the beginning and end of the stitching. Repeat until all the horizontal edges of the motifs are joined.

STEP 3

Turn the work so the remaining edges of the motifs are now horizontal. Working in the same way as above, join the remaining edges together with horizontal rows of overcasting. When working the corners, take the needle under the stitch made on the previous row.

SEWING THROUGH BOTH LOOPS

To make a stronger but slightly less neat join than the one shown above, work in the same way, but insert the needle through both loops of the motif edges.

JOINING WITH SLIPSTITCH

STEP 1

Joining motif edges by slipstitching them together with a crochet hook makes a firm seam with an attractive ridge on the right side. Lay the motifs out as above and work all the horizontal seams first. Place the first two motifs together, wrong sides facing, and work a row of slipstitch (page 19) through both loops of each motif.

STEP 2

When you reach the corner, align the next two motifs, carry the thread firmly across and join them together in the same way. Continue joining motifs along the row, keeping your tension even. Secure the thread ends carefully, then repeat until all the horizontal edges of the motifs are joined.

JOINING WITH DOUBLE CROCHET

STEP 1

Double crochet (page 19) can also be used to join edges together, but it makes a thick seam which looks neatest when the stitches are worked on the wrong side of the work. Work as for slipstitch joins (left), but place the motifs right sides together and work rows of double crochet through both loops of the motif edges.

STEP 3

Turn the work so the remaining edges of the motifs are now horizontal. Working in the same way as above, join the remaining edges together with horizontal rows of slipstitch. When working the corners, carry the thread firmly across the ridge.

STEP 2

To make a less heavy double crochet seam, place the motifs right sides together and work the rows of double crochet stitches through the back loops only.

PROJECT 5 | BABY AFGHAN

Quick to make in traditional granny squares, this baby afghan is the classic gift to make for a new baby. Made in an easy-care yarn, the afghan will come up fresh as a daisy after it is machine washed.

SPECIAL TECHNIQUES USED
Working in rounds (page 56-60)
Joining new yarn (page 28)
Joining square motifs (page 61-63)

CHECK YOUR TENSION
Make one motif. Pin out and block the sample by spraying with water, allow to dry, and measure. The motifs should be approx 12.5 cm (5 in.) square.

If you have a smaller motif, your tension is too tight and you should make another sample using a larger hook.

If you have a larger motif, your tension is too loose and you should make another sample using a smaller hook.

ABBREVIATIONS
ch—chain; **dc**—double crochet; **tr**—treble crochet; **sl st**—slipstitch; **sp**—space; **rep**—repeat

SIZE
76 x 101.5 cm (30 x 40 in.) (6 x 8 squares)

MATERIALS
QUANTITY 1 x 50 g ball of A and B, 2 x 50 g balls of C and D, 3 x 50 g balls of E

YARN "Snuggly Double Knitting" by Sirdar (or DK weight baby yarn with approx 175 m/191 yd per 50 g ball)

COLOUR 374 Violet (A), 216 Sky (B), 341 Blueberry (C), 202 Blush Pink (D), 382 Buttermilk (E)

HOOK SIZE 3.5 mm (Size E)

NEEDLE Large tapestry needle

TIP
Avoid pressing synthetic yarns if possible. Block the motifs by pinning each one out to size and spraying lightly with cold water. Allow the yarn to dry completely before removing the pins. After machine washing, gently pull the afghan into shape along the seams, and tumble or line dry.

NOTES
Always read all the way through the pattern before you begin and make sure that you understand the techniques involved.

Working the motifs

Using yarn A, 6 ch and join with sl st to form a ring.

Round 1 3 ch (counts as 1 tr), 2 tr into ring, 3 ch, * 3 tr into ring, 3 ch; rep from * twice more, sl st into 3rd of 3 ch.

Break off yarn A.

Round 2 Join yarn B to 3 ch sp, 3 ch (counts as 1tr), [2 tr, 3 ch, 3 tr] into same sp to make corner, * 1 ch, [3 tr, 3 ch, 3 tr] into next 3 ch sp to make corner; rep from * twice more, 1 ch, sl st into 3rd of 3 ch.

Break off yarn B.

ALTERNATIVE SWATCH
It's easy to change the colour scheme on this type of design if you prefer a brighter or more subtle effect. For this sample, we used two strong colours for the first 4 rounds, then finished by working the last 2 rounds in a lighter shade of one of the colours.

Round 3 Join yarn C to corner sp, 3 ch (counts as 1 tr), [2 tr, 3 ch, 3 tr] into same sp, * 1 ch, 3 tr into 1 ch sp, 1 ch, [3 tr, 3 ch, 3 tr] into corner sp; rep from * to end, ending with 1 ch, sl st into 3rd of 3 ch.

Break off yarn C.

Round 4 Join yarn D to corner sp, 3 ch (counts as 1 tr), [2 tr, 3 ch, 3 tr] into same sp, * [1 ch, 3 tr into each 1ch sp] along side of square, ch 1, [3 tr, 3 ch, 3 tr] into corner sp; rep from * to end, ending with 1 ch, sl st into 3rd of 3 ch.

Break off yarn D.

Round 5 Join yarn E to corner sp, 3 ch (counts as 1 tr), [2 tr, 3 ch, 3 tr] into same sp, * [1 ch, 3 tr into each 1 ch sp] along side of square, 1 ch, [3 tr, 3 ch, 3 tr] into corner sp; rep from * to end, ending with 1 ch, sl st into 3rd of 3 ch.

Round 6 1 ch, work 1 dc into every tr and 1 ch sp, working [2 dc, 1 ch, 2 dc] into each corner space, join with sl st into first dc.

Fasten off yarn E.

Finishing

Weave in the short yarn ends, block each piece (page 34), and allow to dry completely.

Arrange the motifs as shown in the diagram. Join together with yarn E using one of the methods shown on page 82.

LACE MOTIFS

Lace motifs are light, pretty and delicate to look at when worked in lightweight yarns, and are perfect for making shawls, wraps, and stoles. Lace motifs are usually joined together on the final pattern round as you work, eliminating the need for sewing. It's usual to join several motifs to make a strip, then add further motifs along one long edge of the strip until you have two strips joined together. Keep adding motifs until you have joined the required number of strips together.

MAKING AND WORKING INTO A CHAIN LOOP

STEP 1 Long chain loops (they may also be described as chain spaces or chain arches) are an integral part of lace motif patterns. They are sometimes used as a foundation for stitches worked in the following round, or they may form a visible part of the design. Work chain loops as evenly as possible, anchoring them by working a slipstitch or double crochet into the previous round.

CHANGING THE HOOK POSITION WITH SLIP STITCHES

Working in slipstitch (page 19) across one or more stitches is a useful way of changing the position of yarn and hook on a round. Pattern directions may refer to this technique as "slipstitch across" or "slipstitch into". Here, slip stitches are being worked into the edge of a petal in order to move the hook and yarn from the valley between two petals to the tip of one petal, ready to work the next sequence of stitches.

STEP 2 When a chain loop is worked as a foundation on one row, stitches are worked over the chains on the following row. Insert the hook into the space below the chain loop to work each stitch, not directly into individual chain stitches.

STEP 2 Place the first and second motifs together, with wrong sides facing, ready to work the next side of the second motif. Join the chain loops with a double crochet stitch, then complete the loop on the second motif. Continue along the same side of the second motif, joining chain loops together with double crochet stitches.

JOINING LACE MOTIFS

STEP 1 Complete the first motif. Work the second motif up to the last round, then work the first side of the last round, ending at the specified point where the first join will be made, in this case halfway along a chain loop at the corner of the motif.

STEP 3 After all the loops along one side are joined, complete the second motif in the usual way. Work further motifs in the same way, joining the required number together to make a strip.

STEP 4
Work the first motif of the second strip, stopping when you have reached the joining point. Place against the side of the top motif in the first strip (wrong sides facing) and join the chain loops as before. When you reach the point where three corner loops meet, work the double crochet into the stitch joining the two existing motifs.

STEP 5
Work the second motif of the second strip, stopping when you have reached the joining point. Place against the side of the first motif in the second strip (wrong sides facing) and join the chain loops as before. When you reach the point where all four corner loops meet, work the double crochet into the stitch joining the first two motifs.

STEP 6
Now join the next side of the motif to the adjacent side of the first strip, working double crochet stitches into chain loops as before. Complete the remaining sides of the motif. Continue working in the same way until you have made and joined the required number of motifs.

LACE MOTIFS PATTERN LIBRARY

LACY FLOWER

Foundation ring 8 ch and join with sl st to form a ring.

Round 1 3 ch (counts as 1 tr), 2 tr into ring, 7 ch, [3 tr, 7 ch] 7 times into ring, join with sl st to 3rd of 3 ch.

Round 2 Sl st across next 2 tr and 2 ch, 3 ch (counts as 1 tr), keeping last loop of each st on hook, work 3 tr into first 7 ch loop, yoh and draw through all loops on hook (3 tr cluster made), * 9 ch, leaving last loop of each st on hook, work 4 tr into next 7 ch loop, yoh and draw through all loops on hook (4 tr cluster made); rep from * 6 times, 9 ch, join with sl st to top of first cluster.

Round 3 * [2 dc, 5 ch, 2 dc] into next 9 ch loop, 7 ch, [4 tr cluster, 5 ch, 4 tr cluster] into next 9 ch loop, 7 ch; rep from * to end of round, join with sl st to first dc.

Round 4 Sl st into next dc and

into next 5 ch loop, 2 dc into same loop, * 5 ch, 2 dc into next 7 ch loop, 5 ch, [4 tr cluster, 5 ch, 4 tr cluster] into next 5 ch loop, 5 ch, 2 dc into 7 ch loop, 5 ch, 2 dc into next 5 ch loop; rep from * to end of round, ending with 5 ch, join with sl st to beg of round.
Fasten off yarn.

Spanish lace

Foundation ring 8 ch and join with sl st to form a ring.

Round 1 2 ch (counts as 1 dc), work 15 dc into ring, join with sl st to 2nd of 2 ch.

Round 2 5 ch (counts as 1 htr, 3 ch), * miss 1 dc, 1 htr into next sc, 3 ch; rep from * 6 times, join with sl st to 2nd of 5 ch.

Round 3 Work [1 dc, 1 htr, 3 tr, 1 htr, 1 dc] into each ch sp, join with sl st to first sc. (8 petals).

Round 4 2 ch, * 2 ch, 1 dc into top of next petal, 6 ch, 1 dc into top of next petal, 3 ch, 1 htr into sp before next dc at beg of next petal, 3 ch, 1 htr into same sp; rep from * twice, 3 ch, 1 dc into top of next petal, 6 ch, 1 dc into top of next petal, 3 ch, 1 htr into sp before dc at beg of next petal, 3 ch, join with sl st to first of 3 ch.

Round 5 * 4 ch, work [3 tr, 3 ch, 3 tr] into 6 ch sp, 4 ch, 1 dc into htr, 1 dc into 3 ch sp, 1 dc into htr; rep from * to end, join with sl st to first of 4 ch.

Round 6 * 5 ch, 1 tr into each of next 3 tr, 5 ch, insert hook into 3rd ch from hook and work 1 dc to make picot, 2 ch, 1 tr into each of next 3 tr, 5 ch, sl st into next dc, 4 ch, insert hook into 3rd ch from hook and work 1 dc to make picot, 1 ch, miss 1 dc, sl st into next dc; rep from * to end, join with sl st to first of 5 ch.
Fasten off yarn.

Sunflower lace

Foundation ring 4 ch and join with sl st to form a ring.

Round 1 2 ch (counts as 1 dc), work 7 dc into ring, join with sl st to first of 2 ch.

Round 2 4 ch (counts as 1 tr, 1 ch), 1 tr into first dc, * 1 ch, 1 tr into next dc; rep from * to end, ending last rep with 1 ch, join with sl st into 3rd ch of 4 ch.

Round 3 3 ch (counts as 1 tr), 3 tr into 1 ch sp, * 1 tr into dc, 3 tr into 1 ch sp; rep from * to end, join with sl st into 3rd of 3 ch.

Round 4 9 ch (counts as 1 dtr, 5 ch), 1 dtr into same place as sl st, * miss 3 tr, [3 dtr, 5 ch, 3 dtr] into next tr, miss 3 tr, [1 dtr, 5 ch, 1 dtr] into next tr; rep from *, ending last rep with miss 3 tr, [3 dtr, 5 ch, 3 dtr] into next tr, miss 3 tr, join with sl st into 4th of 9 ch.

Round 5 Sl st over first 2 ch, 1 dc into 3rd ch, 7 ch, * [3 dtr, 5 ch, 3 dtr] into 5 ch sp, 7 ch, 1 dc into centre of foll 5 ch sp, 7 ch; rep from *, ending last rep with [3 dtr, 5 ch, 3 dtr] into 5 ch sp, 7 ch, join with sl st into first dc.
Fasten off yarn.

LACE EVENING WRAP

Light and lacy motifs are worked in a luxurious silk yarn to make this delightful evening wrap. The lace motifs are joined together as you go and the outside of the wrap is trimmed with a neat edging.

SIZE

61 x 183 cm (24 x 72 in.) (6 x 18 motifs)

MATERIALS

QUANTITY 8 x 50 g balls

YARN "Silk 4Ply" by Jaeger (or 4ply silk yarn with approx 192 m/210 yd per 50 g ball)

COLOUR 144 Brilliant

HOOK SIZE 3 mm (C)

NEEDLE Large tapestry needle

SPECIAL TECHNIQUES USED

Working in the round (page 56–60)

Working a lace motif (page 66)

Joining lace motifs together (page 67)

CHECK YOUR TENSION

Make one motif. Pin out and block the sample (page 34), allow to dry, and measure. Measured across the square from picot to picot, the motif should be 10 cm (4 in.) square.

If you have a smaller motif, your tension is too tight and you should make another sample using a larger hook.

If you have a larger motif, your tension is too loose and you should make another sample using a smaller hook.

ABBREVIATIONS

sl st— slipstitch; **ch**—chain; **dc**—double crochet; **htr**—half treble crochet; **tr**—treble crochet; **sp**—space; **st(s)**—stitch(es); **rep**—repeat

TIP

When working with a soft, slippery yarn such as pure silk or a viscose blend, take special care to fasten off all the yarn ends securely on the wrong side to prevent them from working loose with wear.

NOTES

Always read all the way through the pattern before you begin and make sure that you understand the techniques involved.

WORKING MOTIF A

7 ch and join with sl st to form a ring.

Round 1 (right side) 3 ch (counts as 1 tr), * 2 ch, 1 tr into ring; rep from * 10 times more, 2 ch, join with sl st to 3rd of 3 ch (12 spaced tr).

Round 2 3 ch (counts as 1 tr), * 3 ch, 1 tr in next tr; rep from * 10 times more, 3 ch, join with sl st to 3rd of 3 ch (12 spaced tr).

Round 3 * Into next 3 ch loop, work 1 dc, 1 htr, 1 tr, 1 htr, 1 dc (1 shell made); rep from * 11 times more, join with sl st into first dc (12 shells).

Round 4 Sl st across next htr and into tr at top of shell, * 7 ch, 1 dc into tr at centre of next shell; rep from * 10 times more, 7 ch, join with sl st into first of 7 ch (12 loops).

Round 5 * Into next loop work 4 dc, 11 ch, 4 dc to form corner, into each of next 2 loops work 4 dc, 3 ch to form picot, 4 dc; rep from * 3 times more, join with sl st to first dc.
Fasten off yarn.

WORKING MOTIF B

Work as given above for motif A until round 4 has been completed, then join one side of motif B to one side of motif A as follows:

Round 5 Work as round 5 of motif A for the first 3 loops, into 4th loop work 4 dc, 5 ch, place WS of both motifs together and join by working 1 dc into 11 ch corner loop of motif A, 5 ch, return to 4th loop of motif B, work another 4 dc to complete corner, * into next loop work 4 dc, 1 ch, 1 dc into corresponding picot of motif A, 1 ch, 4 dc into same loop of motif B, rep from * once more, then into next corner loop of motif B work 4 dc, 5 ch, 1 dc into 11 ch corner loop of motif A, 5 ch, another 4 dc into same loop of motif B to complete corner, work remainder of motif as given for motif A.
Fasten off yarn.

ALTERNATIVE SWATCH
The silk yarn used for this project is a standard 4ply thickness, which means that you can substitute a less expensive yarn such as cotton, wool or a synthetic blend of the same weight. The sample shown here is made from pure cotton yarn in a similar colour. You may need to adjust the quantity you buy because cotton is heavier than silk and has a shorter yardage per ball – see page 10 for help with estimating yarn amounts.

Working in this way, join 4 more motifs (C, D, E, F) to A and B to make a strip of 6 joined motifs. Work the top motif of the second strip (G) in the same way as motif B, joining it to the side edge of motif A.

Working motif H

Round 5 (to work loops 1, 2, 3) Work as round 5 of the first motif for the first 3 loops.

Round 5 (to join loops 4, 5, 6) Into 4th loop work 4 dc, 5 ch, place WS of motif G and motif H together and join by working 1 dc into 11 ch corner loop of motif G, 5 ch, return to 4th loop of motif H, work another 4 dc to complete corner, * into next loop work 4 dc, 1 ch, 1 dc into corresponding picot of motif G, 1 ch, 4 dc into same loop of motif H, rep from * once more.

Round 5 (to join loops 7, 8, 9) Into next corner loop of motif H work 4 dc, 5 ch, 1 dc into 11 ch corner loop of motif G, 5 ch, another 4 dc into same loop of motif H to complete corner, place WS of motif B and motif H together, * into next loop of motif H work 4 dc, 1 ch, 1 dc into corresponding picot of motif B, 1 ch, 4 dc into same loop of motif H, rep from * once more.

Round 5 (to work loops 10, 11, 12) Into next corner loop of motif H work 4 dc, 5 ch, 1 dc into 11 ch corner loop of motif B, 5 ch, another 4 dc into same loop of motif H to complete corner. Work remainder of motif as given for motif A. Fasten off yarn.

Working in this way, join 4 more motifs (I, J, K, L) together to complete the 2nd strip. Continue adding strips of motifs, starting at the top of each strip and working in the same way until you have 18 strips of motifs joined together.

Working the edging

With the RS of the scarf facing, join the yarn to the first 3 ch sp on the top long edge.

Round 1 1 ch, 1 dc into same sp, * 6 ch, 1 dc into next 3 ch sp, 9 ch, 1 dc where 11 ch loops meet, 9 ch, 1 dc into next 3 ch sp; rep from * to end, working [9 ch, 1 dc into 11 ch loop, 9 ch] into single 11 ch loop at each corner, join with sl st to first dc.

Round 2 1 ch, * 6 dc into 6 ch loop, 1 dc into next dc, 9 dc into 9 ch loop, 1 dc into next dc twice; rep from * to end, working 3 dc into dc at each corner, join with sl st into first ch.
Fasten off yarn.

Finishing

Weave in the short yarn ends. Working in sections, pin out the wrap following the instructions on page 34. Spray the pinned section lightly with cold water. Allow each section to dry thoroughly before removing the pins and moving onto the next section.

SHAPED MOTIFS

Hexagonal, triangular and octagonal motifs are worked in a similar way to circular and square motifs (pages 56–60), but have different sequences of increases to make the six, three or eight corners required. Hexagonal motifs are joined edge to edge to make large pieces of crochet such as afghans, as are triangular motifs, but octagonal motifs need the addition of small square motifs to fill in the gaps between the edges of the octagons.

Join shaped motifs with solidly worked last rounds together by using any of the sewn or crocheted methods described on pages 61–63. You won't be able to join shaped motifs in the long horizontal rows used for square motifs. Instead, lay the pieces out in the required arrangement and join the edges that touch with separate seams. Pay special attention to securing the yarn ends neatly at the beginning and end of each seam. Crochet the edges of lacy shaped motifs (or motifs with picots around the edges such as the Picot Octagon on page 77 and its related joining square) together on the last round using the method shown on pages 67–68.

HEXAGONAL MOTIFS PATTERN LIBRARY

WHEEL HEXAGON

Foundation ring 6 ch and join with sl st to form a ring.

Round 1 6 ch (counts as 1 dtr, 2 ch), 1 dtr into ring, * 2 ch, 1 dtr into ring; rep from * 9 times, 2 ch, join with sl st into 4th of 6 ch. (12 spaced tr).

Round 2 Sl st into next 2 ch sp, 3 ch (counts as 1 tr), [1 tr, 2 ch, 2 tr] into same 2 ch sp as sl st, * 3 tr into next 2 ch sp, [2 tr, 2 ch, 2 tr] into next 2 ch sp; rep from * 4 times, 3 tr into next 2 ch sp, join with sl st into 3rd of 3 ch.

Round 3 3 ch (counts as 1 tr), 1 tr into next tr, [2 tr, 3 ch, 2 tr] into 2 ch sp, 1 tr into each of next 7 tr, * [2 tr, 2 ch, 2 tr] into next 2 ch sp, 1 tr into each of next 7 tr; rep from * 4 times, ending last rep with 1 tr into each of next 5 tr, join with sl st into 3rd of 3 ch.
Fasten off yarn.

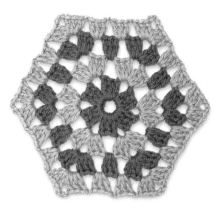

Granny hexagon

Foundation ring Using yarn A, 8 ch and join with sl st to form a ring.

Round 1 3 ch (counts as 1 tr), 2 tr into ring, 3 ch, * 3 tr into ring, 3 ch; rep from * 4 times, join with sl st into 3rd of 3 ch. Break off yarn A.

Round 2 Join yarn B to 3 ch sp, 3 ch (counts as 1 tr), [2 tr, 3 ch, 3 tr] into same sp to make corner, * 1 ch, [3 tr, 3 ch, 3 tr] into next 3 ch sp to make corner; rep from * 4 times, 1 ch, join with sl st into 3rd of 3 ch. Break off yarn B.

Round 3 Join yarn A to corner sp, 3 ch, [2 tr, 3 ch, 3 tr] into same sp, † 1 ch, 3 tr into 1 ch sp, 1 ch, [3 tr, 3 ch, 3 tr] into corner sp; rep from † 4 times, 1 ch, 3 tr into 1 ch sp, 1 ch, join with sl st into 3rd of 3 ch. Break off yarn A.

Round 4 Join yarn B to corner sp, 3 ch, [2 tr, 3 ch, 3 tr] into same sp, † [1 ch, 3 tr into each 1 ch sp] along side of hexagon, 1 ch, [3 tr, 3 ch, 3 tr] into corner sp; rep from † 4 times, [1 ch, 3 tr into each 1 ch sp] along side of hexagon, 1 ch, join with sl st into 3rd of 3 ch.
Fasten off yarn.

Flower hexagon

Foundation ring Using yarn A, 6 ch and join with sl st to form a ring.

Round 1 (right side) 4 ch (counts as 1 dtr), 2 dtr into ring, 1 ch, * 3 dtr into ring, 1 ch; rep from * 4 times, join with sl st into 4th of 4 ch.

Round 2 Turn work (wrong side). Work * 1 dc into first 1 ch sp, 7 ch; rep from * 5 times, join with sl st into first dc. Break off yarn A.

Round 3 Turn work (right side). Join yarn B to 7 ch lp, [1 htr, 2 tr, 3 dtr, 2 tr, 1 htr] into each 7 ch lp to make petal, join with sl st into first htr. Break off yarn B.

Round 4 Join yarn A to last htr of petal. 4 ch (counts as 1 dtr), work 1 dtr into each htr, 1 tr into each tr, 1 htr into each dtr made on previous row, join with sl st into 4th of 4 ch.
Fasten off yarn.

Textured hexagon

Foundation ring 6 ch and join with sl st to form a ring.

Round 1 1 ch, work 12 dc into ring, join with sl st into first dc.

Round 2 5 ch (counts as 1 tr, 2 ch), miss first dc, [1 tr into next dc, 2 ch] 11 times, join with sl st into 3rd of 5 ch.

Round 3 Sl st into first 2 ch sp, 3 ch (counts as 1 tr), 4 tr into same 2 ch sp as sl st, drop loop from hook, insert hook into top of 3 ch, pick up dropped loop and draw through, 1 ch to secure (counts as first popcorn), 3 ch, [1 popcorn into next 2 ch sp, 3 ch] 11 times, join with sl st into top of first popcorn.

Round 4 Sl st into first 3 ch sp, 3 ch (counts as 1 tr), 3 tr into same 3 ch sp as sl st, 1 ch, [4 tr into next 3 ch sp, 1 ch] 11 times, join with sl st to 3rd of 3 ch.

Round 5 Sl st into each of next 3 tr and into next 1 ch sp, 3 ch (counts as 1 tr), 3 tr into same 1 ch sp as sl st, 2 ch, [3 tr, 3 ch, 3 tr] into next 1 ch sp, * 2 ch, 4 tr into next 1 ch sp, 2 ch, [3 tr, 3 ch, 3 tr] into next 1 ch sp; rep from * 4 times, 2 ch, join with sl st into 3rd of 3 ch.
Fasten off yarn.

Round 1 4 ch (counts as 1 tr, 1 ch), [1 tr into ring, 1 ch] 11 times, join with sl st into 3rd of 4 ch. (12 spaced tr).

Round 2 3 ch (counts as 1 tr), 2 tr into 1 ch sp, 1 tr into next tr, 2 ch, * 1 tr into next tr, 2 tr into 1 ch sp, 1 tr into next tr, 2 ch; rep from * 4 times, join with sl st into 3rd of 3 ch. Break off yarn A.

Round 3 Using yarn B, 3 ch (counts as 1 tr), 1 tr into same place, 1 tr into each of next 2 tr, 2 tr into next tr, 2 ch, * 2 tr into next tr, 1 tr into each of next 2 tr, 2 tr into next tr, 2 ch; rep from * 4 times, join with

sl st into 3rd of 3 ch. Break off yarn B.

Round 4 Using yarn A, 3 ch (counts as 1 tr), 1 tr into same place, 1 tr into each of next 4 tr, 2 tr into next tr, 2 ch, * 2 tr into next tr, 1 tr into each of next 4 tr, 2 tr into next tr, 2 ch; rep from * 4 times, join with sl st into 3rd of 3 ch.

Round 5 1 ch, 1 dc into same place, work 1 dc into each tr around hexagon and [2 dc, 1 ch, 2 dc] into each 2 ch sp, join with sl st into first dc.
Fasten off yarn.

STRIPED HEXAGON

Foundation ring Using yarn A, 6 ch and join with sl st to form a ring.

TRIANGULAR MOTIFS PATTERN LIBRARY

FRETWORK TRIANGLE

Foundation ring 6 ch and join with sl st to form a ring.

Round 1 1 ch, work 12 dc into ring, join with sl st into first dc.

Round 2 10 ch (counts as 1 tr, 7 ch), miss first 2 dc, * 1 tr into next dc, 3 ch, miss 1 dc, 1 tr into next dc, 7 ch, miss 1 dc; rep from * once, 1 tr into next dc, 3 ch, miss last dc, join with sl st into 3rd of 10 ch. (6 spaced tr).

Round 3 3 ch (counts as 1 tr), [3 tr, 7 ch, 4 tr] into next 7 ch sp, * 3 dc into next 3 ch sp,

[4 tr, 7 ch, 4 tr] into next 7 ch sp; rep from * once, 3 tr into 3 ch sp, join with sl st into 3rd of 3 ch.

Round 4 6 ch (counts as 1 tr, 3 ch), * [4 tr, 5 ch, 4 tr] into next 7 ch sp, 3 ch, miss 2 tr, 1 tr into next tr, 3 ch, miss 2 tr, 1 tr into next tr, 3 ch, † miss 2 tr, 1 tr into next tr, 3 ch; rep from * once and from * to † once, join with sl st into 3rd of 6 ch.

Round 5 1 ch, work 1 dc in each tr around triangle, working 3 tr into each 3 ch sp and 5 tr into each 5 ch sp, join with sl st into first dc.
Fasten off yarn.

CATHEDRAL TRIANGLE

Foundation ring 6 ch and join with sl st to form a ring.

Round 1 3 ch (counts as 1 tr), work 14 tr into ring, join with sl st into 3rd of 3 ch. (15 tr).

Round 2 3 ch (counts as 1 tr), 1 tr into each of next 4 tr, 5 ch, [1 dc into each of next 5 tr, 5 ch] twice, join with sl st into 3rd of 3 ch.

Round 3 3 ch (counts as 1 tr), 1 tr into each of next 4 tr, [5 tr, 3 ch, 5 tr] into 5 ch sp, * 1 tr into each of next 5 tr, [5 tr, 3 ch, 5 tr] into 5 ch sp; rep from * to end, join with sl st into 3rd of 3 ch.

Round 4 3 ch (counts as 1 tr), work 1 tr into each tr around triangle, working [3 tr, 1 ch, 3 tr] into each 3 ch sp, join with sl st into 3rd of 3 ch.
Fasten off yarn.

OCTAGONAL MOTIFS PATTERN LIBRARY

STRIPED OCTAGON

Foundation ring Using yarn A, 5 ch and join with sl st to form a ring.

Round 1 3 ch (counts as 1 tr), work 15 tr into ring, join with sl st into 3rd of 3 ch. (16 tr). Break off yarn A.

Round 2 Using yarn B, 3 ch (counts as 1 tr), 2 tr in base of ch, * 1 tr into next tr, 3 tr into next tr; rep from * 6 times, 1 tr into next tr, join with sl st into 3rd of 3 ch. Break off yarn B.

Round 3 Using yarn A, 3 ch (counts as 1 tr), * 3 tr into next tr, 1 tr into each of next 3 tr; rep from * 6 times, 3 tr into next tr, 1 tr into each of next 2 tr, join with sl st into 3rd of 3 ch. Break off yarn A.

Round 4 Using yarn B, 3 ch (counts as 1 tr), 1 tr into next tr, * 3 tr into next tr, 1 dc into each of next 5 tr; rep from * 6 times, 3 tr into next tr, 1 tr into each of next 3 tr, join with sl st into 3rd of 3 ch. (64 tr).
Fasten off yarn.

STRIPED JOINING SQUARE

Foundation ring Using yarn A, 5 ch and join with sl st to form a ring.

Round 1 3 ch (counts as 1 tr), work 15 tr into ring, join with sl st into 3rd of 3 ch. (16 tr). Break off yarn A.

Round 2 Using yarn B, 1 ch, 1 dc into same place, 1 dc into each of next 3 tr, 2 ch, [1 dc into each of next 4 tr, 2 ch] 3 times, join with sl st into first dc.

Round 3 1 ch, 1 dc into same place, 1 dc into each of next 3 dc, 5 dc into 2 ch sp, [1 dc into each of next 4 dc, 5 dc into 2 ch sp] 3 times, join with sl st into first dc.
Fasten off yarn.

PICOT OCTAGON

Foundation ring 8 ch and join with sl st to form a ring.

Round 1 3 ch (counts as 1 tr), work 15 tr into ring, join with sl st into 3rd of 3 ch. (16 tr).

Round 2 5 ch (counts as 1 tr, 2 ch), [1 tr, 2 ch] into each tr, join with sl st into 3rd of 3 ch. (16 spaced tr).

Round 3 Sl st into next 2 ch sp, 3 ch (counts as 1 tr), 2 tr into same 2 ch sp, 3 tr into next 3 ch sp, 3 ch, [3 tr into next

2 ch sp] twice, 3 ch; rep from * 6 times, join with sl st into 3rd of 3 ch.

Round 4 1 ch, 1 dc into same place, 1 dc into each of next 5 tr, [2 dc, 3 ch, 2 dc] into 3 ch sp, * 1 dc into each of next 6 tr, [2 dc, 3 ch, 2 dc] into 3 ch sp; rep from * to end, join with sl st into first dc.
Fasten off yarn.

PICOT JOINING SQUARE

Foundation ring 8 ch and join with sl st to form a ring.

Round 1 3 ch (counts as 1 tr), work 15 tr into ring, join with sl st into 3rd of 3 ch. (16 tr).

Round 2 1 ch, 1 sc into same place, 1 sc into each of next 3 dc, 3 ch, [1 dc into each of next 4 dc, 3 ch] 3 times, join with sl st into first dc.

Round 3 1 ch, 1 dc into same place, 1 dc into each of next 3 dc, [2 dc, 3 ch, 2 dc] into 3 ch sp, * 1 dc into each of next 4 dc, [2 dc, 3 ch, 2 dc] into 3 ch sp; rep from * twice, join with sl st into first dc.
Fasten off yarn.

HARLEQUIN AFGHAN

Twenty colours of yarn are combined to make this wonderfully warm afghan. Worked in full and half hexagons, plain and striped motifs are joined together as you work, with motifs and colours arranged randomly to make your afghan into something totally unique. The edge is finished with a neat, three-colour striped edging.

SIZE

101.5 cm (40 in.) wide, 140 cm (55 in.) long, including edging

MATERIALS

QUANTITY 1 x 50 g ball of each colour

YARN "Matchmaker Merino Double Knitting" by Jaeger (or pure wool DK yarn with approx 120 m/131 yd per 50 g ball)

COLOUR 662 Cream, 663 Light Natural, 784 Oatmeal, 639 Granite, 868 Raspberry, 883 Petal, 888 Parma, 885 Oyster, 884 Seafoam, 879 Nantucket, 886 Asparagus, 626 Dusk, 887 Fuchsia, 862 Butter, 857 Sage, 856 Buddleia, 889 Pacific, 863 Down, 870 Rosy, 881 Trellis

HOOK SIZE 3.5 mm (E)

SPECIAL TECHNIQUES USED

Working in the round (page 56-60)
Working a shaped motif (page 74-77)
Joining motifs as you go (page 61-63)
Working a decrease in double crochet (page 52)

CHECK YOUR TENSION

Make one hexagon motif. Pin out and block (page 34), allow to dry, and measure. Measured across the center from side to side of the hexagon, the motif should be 14 cm (5½ in.) across.

If you have a smaller motif, your tension is too tight and you should make another sample using a larger hook.

If you have a larger motif, your tension is too loose and you should make another sample using a smaller hook.

ABBREVIATIONS

sl st—slipstitch; **ch**—chain; **dc**—double crochet; **tr**—treble crochet; **sp**—space; **st(s)**—stitch(es); **rep**—repeat; **WS**—wrong side; **tog**—together

Special Abbreviation for this Pattern
dc2tog = work 2 double crochet stitches together

TIP

Be as adventurous as you like mixing and matching the colours and the plain and striped hexagons when you're joining them together – don't forget that there are no right or wrong colour combinations in this pattern, just ones that you like.

NOTES

1. Always read all the way through the pattern before you begin and make sure that you understand the techniques involved.
2. The full hexagon motifs and the edging are worked in rounds; the half hexagon motifs are worked in rows.

Working hexagon A

Using one colour of yarn, 6 ch and join with sl st to form a ring.

Round 1 (right side) 4 ch (counts as 1 tr, 1 ch), [1tr into ring, 1 ch] 11 times, join with sl st into 3rd of 4 ch (12 spaced tr).

Round 2 3 ch (counts as 1 tr), 2 tr into 1 ch sp, 1 tr into next tr, 2 ch, * 1 dc into next tr, 2 tr into 1 ch sp, 1 tr into next tr, 2 ch; rep from * 4 times, join with sl st to 3rd of 3 ch.

Round 3 3 ch, 1 tr into same place, 1 tr into each of next 2 tr, 2 tr into next tr, 2 ch, * 2 tr into next tr, 1 tr into each of next 2 tr, 2 tr into next tr, 2 ch; rep from * 4 times, join with sl st to 3rd of 3 ch.

Round 4 3 ch, 1 tr into same place, 1 tr into each of next 4 tr, 2 tr into next tr, 2 ch, * 2 tr into next tr, 1 tr into each of next 4 tr, 2 tr into next tr, 2 ch; rep from * 4 times, join with sl st to 3rd of 3 ch.

Round 5 3 ch, 1 tr into each of next 7 tr, * 3 ch, 1 dc into 2 ch sp, 3 ch, 1 tr into each of next 8 tr; rep from * 4 times, 3 ch, 1 dc into 2 ch sp, 3 ch, join with sl st to 3rd of 3 ch.

Round 6 Sl st into next tr, 3 ch, 1 tr into each of next 5 tr, * 3 ch, [1 dc into 3 ch sp, 3 ch] twice, miss next tr, 1 tr into each of next 6 tr; rep from * 4 times, 3 ch, [1 dc into 3 ch sp, 3 ch] twice, join with sl st to 3rd of 3 ch.

Round 7 Sl st into next tr, 3 ch, 1 tr into each of next 3 tr, * 3 ch [1 dc into 3 ch sp, 3 ch] 3 times, miss next tr, 1 tr into each of next 4 tr; rep from * 4 times, 3 ch, [1 dc into 3 ch sp, 3 ch] 3 times, join with sl st to 3rd of 3 ch.

Round 8 Sl st between 2nd and 3rd tr of group, 4 ch (counts as 1 tr, ch 1), 1 tr into same place, * 3 ch, [1 dc into 3 ch sp, 3 ch] 4 times, [1 tr, 1 ch, 1 tr] between 2nd and 3rd tr of group; rep from * 4 times, 3 ch, [1 dc into 3 ch sp, 3 ch] 4 times, join with sl st to 3rd of 4 ch.
Fasten off yarn.

Working hexagon B

Using a different colour of yarn, work as given above for hexagon A until round 7 has been completed, then join one side of hexagon B to one side of hexagon A as follows:

Round 8 Work as round 8 above for the first side, work first tr of corner, place WS of both hexagons together and join by working 1 dc into 1 ch sp of hexagon A, return to hexagon B and work 1 tr to complete corner. Continue along second side of hexagon B, joining the 3 ch loops between each dc by working [1 ch, 1 dc into loop of hexagon A, 1 ch]. At the corner, work first tr, 1 dc into 1 ch sp of hexagon A, 1 tr to complete corner, then work remainder of motif as given for hexagon A.
Fasten off yarn.

Working hexagon C

Using a different colour of yarn, work as given above for hexagon A until round 7 has been completed, then join two sides of hexagon C to one side of hexagon A and one side of hexagon B as follows:

Round 8 Work as round 8 above for the first side, work first tr of corner, place WS of hexagons C and A together and join along one side by working 1 dc into 1 ch sp of hexagon A, return to hexagon C and work 1 tr to complete corner. Continue along second side of hexagon C, joining the 3 ch loops between each dc by working [1 ch, 1 dc into loop of hexagon A, 1 ch]. At the corner, work first tr, 1 dc into 1 ch sp of hexagon A, 1 dc into 1 ch sp of hexagon B, 1 tr to complete corner, then join the next side of hexagon C to hexagon B in the same way as above, working remainder of hexagon C as given for hexagon A.
Fasten off yarn.

Working the remaining full hexagons

Working in the same way, make and join together an additional 69 hexagons, arranging the colours at random. Build outwards from the first 3 motifs, joining the corners and 3 ch loops of adjacent sides as above. All 72 full hexagons are shown on the diagram.

Colour variations for striped hexagons

There are four striped variations of the full hexagon motif dotted at random across the afghan. You can, if you prefer, work more or less of these variations than on the afghan shown in the photograph.

Hexagon with contrasting centre: Work the ring and round 1 in a contrasting colour.

Hexagon with contrasting outer ring: Work rounds 6 and 7 in a contrasting colour.

Hexagon with single stripe: Work round 5 in a contrasting colour.

Three-colour hexagon: Work the ring, rounds 1 and 2 in one colour; rounds 3 and 4 in a second colour; rounds 5 to 8 in a third colour.

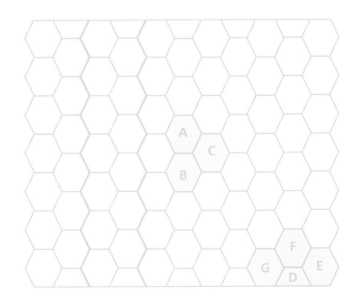

WORKING THE HALF HEXAGONS

When all 72 full hexagons have been made and joined together, you will need to make 10 half hexagons to fill the spaces along the top and bottom edges. The half hexagons are worked in rows instead of rounds and are then joined to three adjacent edges of the full hexagons as follows:

Using one colour of yarn, ch 6 and join with sl st to form a ring.

Row 1 (right side) 4 ch (counts as 1 tr, 1 ch), [1 tr into ring, 1 ch] 4 times, 1 tr into ring, turn.

Row 2 3 ch (counts as 1 tr), 1 tr into same place, 2 ch, [1 tr into next tr, 2 tr into 1 ch sp, 1 tr into next tr, 2 ch] twice, 2 tr into 3rd of 4 ch, turn.

Row 3 3 ch, 2 tr into next tr, 2 ch, [2 tr into next next tr, 1 tr into each of next 2 tr, 2 tr into next tr, 2 ch] twice, 2 tr into next tr, 1 tr into 3rd of 3 ch, turn.

Row 4 3 ch, 1 tr into next tr, 2 tr into next tr, 2 ch, [2 tr into next tr, 1 tr into each of next 4 tr, 2 tr into next tr, 2 ch] twice, 2 tr into next tr, 1 tr into next tr, 1 tr into 3rd of 3 ch, turn.

Row 5 3 ch, 1 tr into each of next 3 tr, 3 ch, 1 dc into 2 ch sp, 3 ch, [1 tr into each of next 8 tr, 3 ch, 1 dc into 2 ch sp, 3 ch] twice, 1 tr into each of next 3 tr, 1 dc into 3rd of 3 ch, turn.

Row 6 3 ch, 1 tr into each of next 2 tr, * 3 ch, [1 dc into 3 ch sp, 3 ch] twice, miss next tr, 1 tr into each of next 6 tr; rep from * once more, 3 ch, [1 dc into 3 ch sp, 3 ch] twice, miss next tr, 1 tr into each of next 2 tr, 1 tr into 3rd of 3 ch, turn.

Row 7 3 ch, 1 tr into next tr, * 3 ch, [1 dc into 3 ch sp, 3 ch] 3 times, miss next tr, 1 tr into each of next 4 tr; rep from * once more, 3 ch, [1 dc into 3 ch sp, 3 ch] 3 times, miss next tr, 1 tr into next tr, 1 tr into 3rd of 3 ch, turn.

Row 8 Place half hexagon (D on diagram) against edge of right-hand hexagon (E on diagram) with WS tog, 1 dc into corner space of E, join the 3 ch loops between each dc by working [1 ch, 1 dc into loop of hexagon E, 1 ch]. At the corner, work first tr, 1 dc into 1 ch sp of hexagon E, 1 dc into 1 ch sp of hexagon F, 1 dc to complete corner.

Working in the same way, join the next side of the half hexagon to hexagon F, work the corner between hexagons F and G, then join the last side of the half hexagon to hexagon G, 1 tr into 3rd of 3 ch.

Fasten off yarn.

Repeat 9 times to make and join the remaining half hexagons.

WORKING THE EDGING

With the RS of the afghan together, join one colour of yarn to the top long edge.

Round 1 1 ch, work a row of dc round the afghan as follows:

Along the straight edges, work 2 dc into each row end of the half hexagons, 3 dc into each 3 ch loop of the full hexagons and 1 dc into each 1 ch sp.

Along the zigzag edges, work 3 dc into each 3 ch loop, [2 dc, 1 ch, 2 dc] into the outer corners and 1 dc into each 1 ch sp at the inner corners.

Join with sl st into first dc.

Fasten off yarn.

Round 2 Join the second colour of yarn, 1 ch, work 1 dc into each dc of previous round, working 3 dc into 1 ch sp at the outer corners and dc2tog at the inner corners, join with sl st to first dc.

Fasten off yarn.

Round 3 Join the third colour of yarn, 1 ch, work 1 dc into each dc of previous round, join with sl st to first dc.

Fasten off yarn.

FINISHING

Weave in the short yarn ends. Press (page 34) the afghan very lightly on the wrong side over a well-padded surface.

FILET CROCHET

Filet crochet is characterized by a mesh background on which the pattern is picked out in solid blocks of stitches. It is always worked from a chart, showing the pattern as it will appear from the right side of the work. The charts are numbered from side to side, reading odd-numbered rows from right to left and even-numbered rows from left to right.

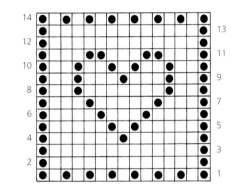

Each open square on a filet crochet chart represents one space – a space is made by working two treble crochet stitches separated by two chains. When a square on the chart is filled in or has a dot or cross in the centre, the chains are replaced by two treble crochet stitches to make a solid block of four stitches. Two blocks together on the chart are filled by seven treble crochet stitches, three blocks by ten stitches, and so on.

Filet crochet charts begin with the first row, so the foundation chain is not shown. To calculate the number of stitches to make, you will need to multiply the number of squares across the chart by 3 and add 1. You will also need to add the correct number of turning chains, depending on whether the first chart row begins with a space or a block (see below).

WORKING THE FIRST ROW

STARTING THE FIRST ROW WITH A SPACE

Make the foundation chain as described above. Start to follow the chart from the bottom right-hand corner, along the row of squares marked 1. When the first square is a space, add 4 turning chains and work the first treble crochet stitch into the 8th chain from the hook. Continue working spaces and blocks along the row, reading the chart from right to left.

STARTING THE FIRST ROW WITH A BLOCK

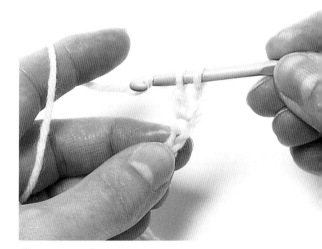

STEP 1 When the first square on the chart is a block, add 2 turning chains and work the first treble crochet stitch into the 4th chain from the hook.

STEP 2
Work 1 treble crochet stitch into each of the next 2 chains to complete the block. Continue along the row, reading the chart from right to left.

WORKING THE REST OF THE CHART ROWS

At the end of the first row, turn the work and follow the second row of the chart, reading from left to right. Work spaces and blocks at the beginning and end of the second and subsequent rows as follows.

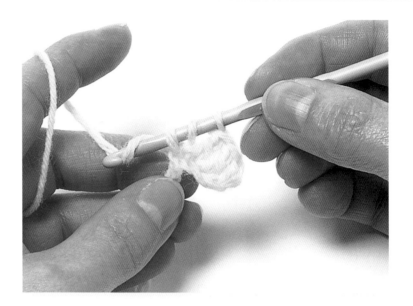

WORKING A SPACE OVER A SPACE ON THE PREVIOUS ROW

STEP 1
At the beginning of a row, work 5 turning chains (counts as 1 treble crochet stitch and 2 chains), miss the first stitch and the next 2 chains, work 1 treble crochet stitch into the next treble, then continue working the spaces and blocks from the chart.

STEP 2
At the end of a row, finish with 1 treble crochet stitch into the last treble crochet, work 2 chains, miss 2 chains, work 1 treble crochet stitch into the third chain of 5 turning chains, turn.

Working a space over a block on the previous row

STEP 1 At the beginning of the row, work 5 turning chains (counts as 1 treble crochet stitch and 2 chains), miss the first 3 stitches, work 1 treble crochet stitch into the next treble crochet, then continue working spaces and blocks from the chart.

STEP 2 At the end of a row, work to the last 4 stitches. Work 1 treble crochet stitch into the next stitch, work 2 chains, miss 2 stitches, work 1 treble crochet stitch into the top chain of 3 turning chains to complete the block, turn.

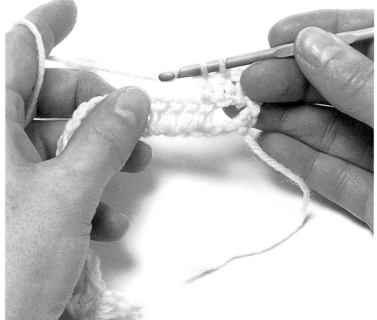

Working a block over a space on the previous row

STEP 1 At the beginning of the row, work 3 turning chains (counts as 1 treble crochet stitch), miss 1 stitch, work 1 treble crochet stitch into each of the next 2 chains, 1 treble crochet stitch into the next stitch to complete the block. Continue across the row working spaces and blocks from the chart.

STEP 2
At the end of a row, finish with 1 treble crochet stitch into the last treble crochet, 1 treble crochet stitch into each of the next 3 chains of the turning chain, turn.

WORKING A BLOCK OVER A BLOCK ON THE PREVIOUS ROW

STEP 1
At the beginning of the row, work 3 turning chains (counts as 1 treble crochet stitch), miss 1 stitch, work 1 treble crochet stitch into each of the next 3 treble crochets to complete the block. Continue across the row working spaces and blocks from the chart.

STEP 2
At the end of a row, finish with 1 treble crochet stitch into each of the last 3 treble crochets, 1 treble crochet stitch into the top chain of 3 turning chains, turn.

SHAPING FILET CROCHET

The shaping is carried out at the beginning and end of the row and makes neat sloping edges to shape sleeves and necklines.

MAKING A SLANTED INCREASE

STEP 1 To increase at the beginning of the row, make 6 turning chains (counts as 1 double treble stitch and 2 chains). Work 1 treble crochet stitch in the same place, then continue along the row.

STEP 2

To increase at the end of the row, work 2 chains, then 1 double treble stitch into the top of the turning chain on the previous row.

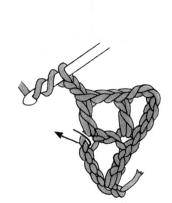

MAKING A SLANTED DECREASE

STEP 1 To decrease at the beginning of the row, work 4 turning chains (counts as 1 double treble stitch), miss the next block or space, work 1 treble crochet stitch into the first stitch of the next space or block.

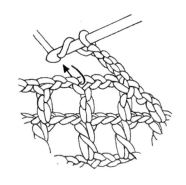

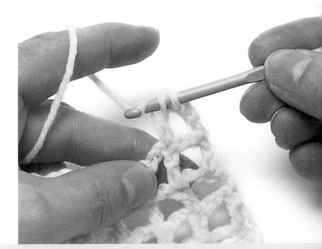

STEP 2 To decrease at the end of the row, work an incomplete treble crochet stitch into the first stitch of the last space or block, leaving 2 loops on the hook. Yarn over hook twice (ready to make a double treble stitch), insert hook into the top of the turning chain on the previous row.

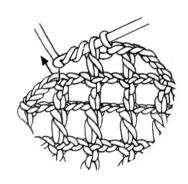

STEP 3 Yarn over hook, pull through one loop on the hook (5 loops on hook), yarn over hook, pull through the first 2 loops on the hook (4 loops on hook).

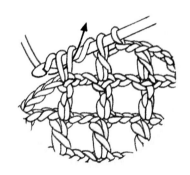

STEP 4 Yarn over hook, pull through 2 loops on hook (3 loops on hook), yarn over hook, pull through the remaining 3 loops to complete the decrease.

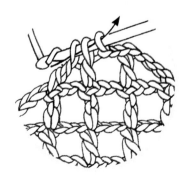

FILET CROCHET TOP

Light and lacy, this filet crochet top is worked in a fine, pure cotton yarn and features a pretty floral border pattern. The fronts and back are worked all in one piece from the lower edge, and the fronts tie loosely with bead-trimmed cords.

SIZES

TO FIT BUST/CHEST	81 [91, 102] cm	
	(32 [36, 40] in.)	
ACTUAL MEASUREMENT	84 [95, 107] cm	
	(33 [37½, 42] in.)	
SIDE LENGTH	25 [28.5, 32] cm	
	(10 [11¼, 12½] in.)	
SLEEVE LENGTH		
(measured straight	38 [41, 44.5] cm	
from top of sleeve	(15 [16¼, 17½] in.)	
to cuff edge)		

MATERIALS

QUANTITY	6 [7, 8] x 50 g balls
YARN	"4ply Cotton" by Rowan (or pure cotton 4ply yarn with approx 170 m/186 yd per 50 g ball)
COLOUR	113 Bleached
HOOK SIZE	2.5 mm, 3 mm (B, C)
NEEDLE	Large tapestry needle

8 Mill Hill Pebble Beads in 5161 Crystal to decorate cords

SPECIAL TECHNIQUES USED

Making a foundation chain (page 17)
Working filet crochet (pages 82–85)
Making slanted increases and decreases in filet crochet (pages 86–87)
Working a double crochet edging (page 37)

CHECK YOUR TENSION

Make a foundation chain of ch 49 and work approximately 15 cm (6 in.) in mesh pattern. Block the sample (pages 34–35), allow to dry and measure the tension (pages 44–45). The recommended tension is 11 spaces to 10 cm (4 in.) measured across the stitches and 12 spaces to 10 cm (4 in.) measured across the rows.

If you have more spaces, your tension is too tight and you should make another sample using a larger hook.

If you have less spaces, your tension is too loose and you should make another sample using a smaller hook.

ABBREVIATIONS

ch—chain; **tr**—treble crochet; **inc**—increase; **st**—stitch; **sp(s)** —space(s)

TIP

• Remember to read all right side rows (odd-numbered rows) from right to left on the charts and all wrong side rows (even-numbered rows) from left to right.
• After making the foundation chain, always begin to work each piece at the bottom right-hand corner of the appropriate chart.

NOTES

1. Always read all the way through the pattern before you begin and make sure that you understand the techniques involved.
2. Figures in brackets [ ] refer to the larger sizes. Where only one figure is given it refers to all sizes.
3. For information on how to work blocks and spaces, refer to the filet crochet section on pages 82–85.

Back & Front (worked in one piece up to armholes)

Using the 3 mm (C) hook, 274 [310, 346] ch plus 4 turning ch.

Change to the 2.5 mm (B) hook.

Row 1 (right side) Start to read the chart from the bottom right-hand corner, along the row of squares marked 1. Work the first tr into the 8th ch from the hook, and continue working spaces along the row. (91 [103, 115] spaces).

Row 2 (wrong side) Turn the work and follow the second row of the chart, reading from left to right. At the beginning of the row, work 5 turning ch (counts as 1 tr, 2 ch), work 1 tr into next tr, then continue working the row from the chart. (91 [103, 115] spaces).

Row 3 & following rows Continue working blocks and spaces from the chart, reading odd-numbered rows from right to left on the charts and even-numbered rows from left to right, until you have worked 28 [32, 36] rows.

Divide for armholes

Right front

Row 29 [33, 37] (right side) Work across the chart until the heavy line is reached. Turn and work only on these stitches to shape the right front. (23 [26, 29] spaces).

Continue working from the chart, and at the same time begin the neck shaping.

Shape neck

Row 31 [35, 39] Decrease the first sp on the row by working a slanted decrease, then work the row from the chart.

Continue working from the chart, decreasing 1 sp at the beginning of every odd-numbered row until 14 [17, 19] spaces remain.

Work even for 3 [3, 3] rows. (14 [17, 19] spaces).

1st size Fasten off yarn.

2nd & 3rd sizes Decrease 1 sp at the beginning of the next row, work straight for 2 [3] rows. (16 [18] spaces).

Fasten off yarn.

Back

With right side facing, rejoin yarn at the bottom of armhole edge of right front, ready to complete the back.

Row 29 [33, 37] Using the 2.5 mm (B) hook, work across the chart from right to left, until the heavy line is reached. (45 [51, 57] spaces).

Turn and work only on these stitches.

Continue working from the chart until all the rows are completed on the back.

Fasten off yarn.

Left front

With right side facing, rejoin yarn at the bottom of left armhole edge of back, ready to work the left front.

Row 29 [33, 37] (right side) Using the 2.5 mm (B) hook, work across the chart until you reach the end of the row. Turn and work only on these stitches to shape the left front. (23 [26, 29] spaces).

Continue working from the chart, and at the same time begin the neck shaping.

ALTERNATIVE SWATCH
Traditionally, filet crochet is worked in fine cotton yarns, usually in white, cream or ecru. This type of crochet also looks light and delicate when worked in fine woollen yarns which make lacy but warm garments for spring and autumn wear.

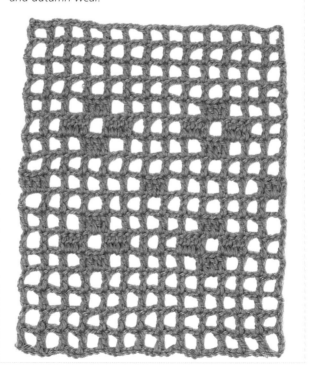

Shape neck

Row 31 [35, 39] Work the row from the chart, decreasing the last sp on the row by working a slanted decrease.

Continue working from the chart, decreasing 1 sp at the end of every odd-numbered row until 14 [17, 19] spaces remain.

Work even for 3 [3, 3] rows. (14 [17, 19] spaces).

1st size Fasten off yarn.

2nd & 3rd sizes Decrease 1 sp at the end of the next row, work straight for 2 [3] rows. (16 [18] spaces).

Fasten off yarn.

Sleeves (make 2)

Using the 3 mm (C) hook, 79 [91, 103] ch plus 4 turning ch.

Change to the 2.5 mm (B) hook.

Row 1 (right side) Start to read the chart from the bottom right-hand corner, along the row of squares marked 1. Work the first tr into the 8th ch from the hook, and continue working spaces along the row. (26 [30, 34] spaces).

Row 2 (wrong side) Turn the work and follow the second row of the chart, reading from left to right. At the beginning of the row, work 5 turning ch (counts as 1 tr, ch 2), work 1 tr into next tr, then continue working the row from the chart. (26 [30, 34] spaces).

Row 3 & following rows Continue working blocks and spaces from the chart, reading odd-numbered rows from right to left on the charts and even-numbered rows from left to right, and at the same time begin the sleeve shaping.

Shape sleeve

Row 4 [4, 4] (wrong side) Work the row from the chart, increasing 1 sp at each end of the row by working a slanted increase.

Continue working from the chart, increasing 1 sp at each end of every 4th row until there are 44 [50, 56] spaces.

Work even for 9 [9, 9] rows. (44 [50, 56] spaces). Fasten off yarn.

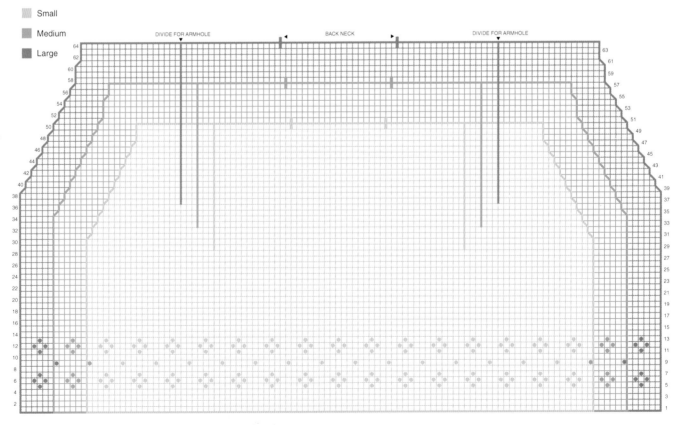

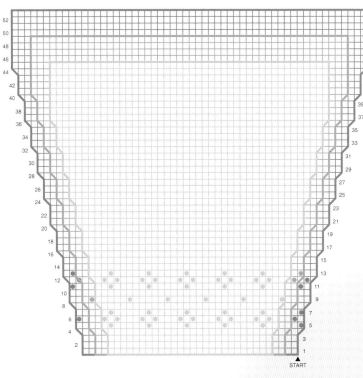

FINISHING

Weave in the short yarn ends, block each piece and allow to dry completely.

With right sides together and beginning at the armhole edges, pin the fronts and back together at the shoulders, aligning the spaces carefully along the seams. Stitch together using the overcasting method on page 62.

Mark the centre point of the sleeves with a pin. With right sides together, join the sleeves to the front and back aligning the spaces at each side of the centre point.

With right sides together and again aligning spaces, join the sleeve and side seams.

WORKING THE EDGING

Using the 3 mm (C) hook, work two rows of double crochet edging (page 37) evenly round the cuffs, neck, front edges and lower edge of the top, fastening off the yarn ends neatly. To make the cords, join the yarn to the wrong side of the edging where the decreasing starts and work a chain to the required length using the 2.5 mm (B) hook. Fasten off the yarn, leaving the ends about 20 cm (8 in.) long. Slide four beads onto each yarn end and knot the end two or three times to hold the beads in position. Trim the yarn ends.

LACE STITCHES

Simple lace stitch patterns are very easy to work, but you should pay special attention to working the correct number of stitches in the foundation chain. For example, the foundation chain for Offset Mesh (page 94) requires a multiple of 2 stitches, so your chain must contain a number of stitches which is divisible by 2.

Some patterns require a multiple of chains, plus a few extra ones which are necessary for the pattern to repeat properly. Plain Trellis (page 94) requires a multiple of 4 stitches plus 2. In this case, your chain must contain a number of stitches which is divisible by 4, then you must add 2 extra chains. For example, a foundation chain of 82 stitches would work for this particular stitch pattern (4 x 20 + 2 = 82).

STEP 2
Work the last treble crochet stitch of each row into the third stitch of the turning chain. This makes a neater, firmer edge than working the stitch into the chain space.

WORKING A TRELLIS PATTERN

Similar to mesh patterns, the chain spaces in trellis patterns are longer, allowing them to curve upwards to create delicate arch-shaped loops. The chain spaces are usually anchored by double crochet stitches worked into the space below each loop.

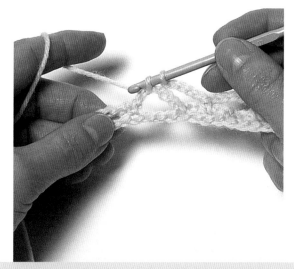

WORKING A SIMPLE MESH PATTERN

STEP 1
Work the treble crochet stitches of simple mesh patterns by inserting the hook into the chain space on the previous row and working the stitch as usual. Don't insert the hook into the chain stitch, but into the space below it.

WORKING A SHELL PATTERN INTO THE FOUNDATION CHAIN

Work the foundation chain as instructed in the pattern, turn and work the first row of the shell pattern straight into the chain. This method gives a narrow edge which is more likely to pull out of shape than the one given below.

WORKING A SHELL PATTERN WITH A FOUNDATION ROW

STEP 1 Work the foundation chain, turn and work the foundation row of the shell pattern into the chain. This method makes a series of chain loops spaced out along the row and gives a stronger, less distorted edge than working the shells straight into the foundation chain.

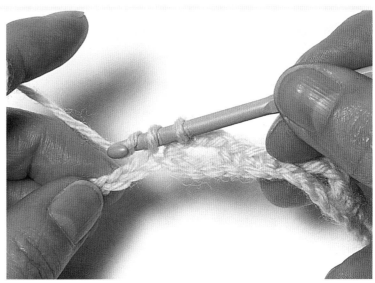

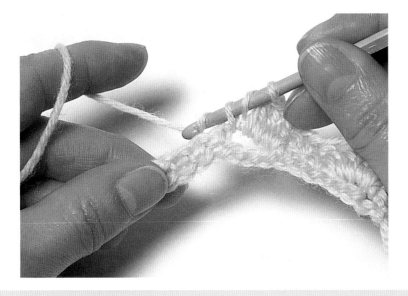

STEP 2 Work the required number of turning chains and turn. Work the first row of shells into the chain loops on the foundation row and continue in pattern.

Lace stitch library

Offset mesh
(RIGHT)

The foundation chain for this pattern requires a multiple of 2 stitches. Make the required length of foundation chain.

Foundation row (right side) 1 tr into 6th ch from hook, * 1 ch, miss 1 ch, 1 tr into next ch; rep from * ending with 1 tr into last ch, turn.

Row 1 4 ch (counts as 1 tr, 1 ch), 1 tr into first 1 ch sp, * 1 ch, miss 1 tr, 1 tr into next 1 ch sp; rep from * to turning ch, 1 tr into 3rd of 4 ch, turn. Rep row 1.

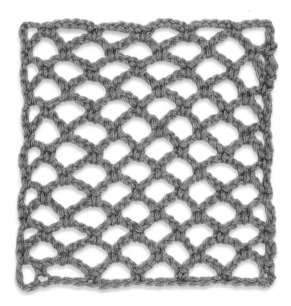

Plain trellis
(LEFT)

The foundation chain for this pattern requires a multiple of 4 stitches plus 2. Make the required length of foundation chain.

Foundation row 1 dc into 6th ch from hook, * 5 ch, miss 3 ch, 1 dc into next ch; rep from * to end, turn.

Row 1 * 5 ch, 1 dc into next 5 ch sp; rep from * to end, turn. Rep row 1.

Picot trellis
(RIGHT)

The foundation chain for this pattern requires a multiple of 5 stitches plus 2. Make the required length of foundation chain.

Foundation row 1 dc into 2nd ch from hook, * 5 ch, miss

4 ch, 1 dc into next ch; rep from * to end, turn.

Row 1 * 5 ch, work a picot of [1 dc, 3 ch, 1 dc] into 3rd ch of next 5 ch loop; rep from * ending with 2 ch, 1 tr into last dc, turn.

Row 2 1 ch, 1 dc into first st, * 5 ch, miss picot, make picot into 3rd ch of next 5 ch loop; rep from * ending with 5 ch, miss picot, 1 dc into arch made by turning ch, turn. Rep rows 1 and 2.

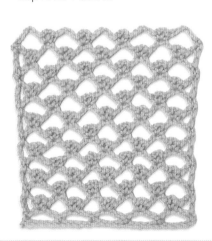

SHELL TRELLIS

The foundation chain for this pattern requires a multiple of 12 stitches plus 3. Make the required length of foundation chain.

Foundation row (right side) 2 tr into 3rd ch from hook, * miss 2 ch, 1 dc into next ch, 5 ch, miss 5 ch, 1 dc into next ch, miss 2 ch, 5 tr into next ch; rep from * ending last rep with only 3 tr into last ch, turn.

Row 1 1 ch, 1 dc into first st, * 5 ch, 1 dc into next 5 ch loop, 5 ch, 1 dc into 3rd tr of next 5 tr; rep from * ending last rep with 1 dc into top of turning ch, turn.

Row 2 * 5 ch, 1 dc into next 5 ch loop, 5 tr into next dc, 1 dc into next 5 ch loop; rep from * ending with 2 ch, 1 tr into last dc, turn.

Row 3 1 ch, 1 dc into first st, * 5 ch, 1 dc into 3rd tr of next 5 tr, 5 ch, 1 dc into next 5 ch loop; rep from * to end, turn.

Row 4 3 ch (counts as 1 tr), 2 tr into first st, * 1 dc into next 5 ch loop, 5 ch, 1 dc into next 5 ch loop, 5 tr into next dc; rep from * ending last rep with only 3 tr into last dc, turn.
Rep rows 1, 2, 3, and 4.

ALTERNATE SHELLS

The foundation chain for this pattern requires a multiple of 6 stitches plus 2. Make the required length of foundation chain.

Foundation row (wrong side) 1 dc into 2nd ch from hook, 1 dc into next ch, * 3 ch, miss 3 ch, 1 dc into each of next 3 ch; rep from * to last 5 ch, 3 ch, miss 3 ch, 1 dc into each of last 2 ch, turn.

Row 1 (right side) 1 ch, 1 dc into first dc, * 5 tr into 3 ch sp, miss 1 dc, 1 dc into next dc; rep from * to end, turn.

Row 2 3 ch, * 1 dc into 2nd, 3rd, and 4th stitches of 5 tr group, 3 ch; rep from * to end, ending with 1 dc into 2nd, 3rd, and 4th stitches of 5 tr group, 2 ch, 1 dc into last st, turn.

Row 3 3 ch, 2 tr into 2 ch sp, miss 1 dc, 1 dc into next dc, * 5 tr into 3 ch sp, miss 1 dc, 1 dc into next dc; rep from * to end, 3 tr into last 3 ch sp, turn.

Row 4 1 ch, 1 dc into each of first 2 tr, * 3 ch, 1 dc into 2nd, 3rd, and 4th stitches of 5 tr group; rep from * to end, ending with 3 ch, 1 dc into 2nd tr, 1 dc into 3rd of 3 ch, turn.
Rep rows 1, 2, 3, and 4.

SMALL SHELLS

The foundation chain for this pattern requires a multiple of 6 stitches plus 4. Make the required length of foundation chain.

Foundation row [1 tr, 3 ch, 1 tr] into 7th ch from hook, * miss 2 ch, [2 tr, 1 ch, 2 tr] into next ch, miss 2 ch, [1 tr, 3 ch, 1 tr] into next ch; rep from * to last 3 ch, miss 2 ch, 1 tr into last ch, turn.

Row 1 3 ch, * [2 tr, 1 ch, 2 tr] into 3 ch sp, [1 tr, 3 ch, 1 tr] into 1 ch sp; rep from * to end, ending with [2 tr, 1 ch, 2 tr] into 3 ch sp, 1 tr into top of turning ch, turn.

Row 2 3 ch, * [1 tr, 3 ch, 1 tr] into 1 ch sp, [2 tr, 1 ch, 2 tr] into 3 ch sp; rep from * to end, ending with [1 tr, 3 ch, 1 tr] into 1 ch sp, 1 tr into turning ch, turn.

Rep rows 1 and 2.

PROJECT 9 LACY SUMMER TOP

Light and lacy, this easy-to-make top is worked in a pure cotton yarn which comes in a wide range of colours. As a great variation, crochet the design using a dark colour of yarn and add sparkling diamanté buttons to make a delightful evening top.

SIZES

to fit bust/chest	81	86	91	cm
	32	34	36	in.
actual measurement	86	91	96	cm
	34	36	38	in.
length to shoulder	39.5	39.5	39.5	cm
	15½	15½	15½	in.

MATERIALS

QUANTITY 5 [6, 6] x 50-g balls

YARN "Cotton Glace" by Rowan (or pure cotton lightweight DK yarn with approx 114 m/125 yd per 50 g ball)

COLOUR Oyster

HOOK SIZE 3.5 mm (E)

NEEDLE Large tapestry needle
Two 1 cm (⅜ in.) diameter buttons
Matching sewing thread
Sewing needle

SPECIAL TECHNIQUES USED

Working a foundation chain (page 16)
Turning chains (page 18)
Working lace patterns (page 68-69)
Edge finishes (page 106-109)

CHECK YOUR TENSION

Make a foundation chain of 34 ch and work approximately 15 cm (6 in.) in pattern, beginning with the foundation row. Block and press the sample, allow to dry, and measure the tension (page 44). The recommended tension is 21 stitches to 10 cm (4 in.) measured across a row of double crochet and 6 cm (2½ in.) across one pattern repeat.

If you have more stitches or a smaller pattern repeat, your tension is too tight and you should make another sample using a larger hook.

If you have less stitches and a larger pattern repeat, your tension is too loose and you should make another sample using a smaller hook.

ABBREVIATIONS

ch—chain; **dc**—double crochet; **htr**—half treble crochet; **tr**—treble crochet; **sp**—space; **incl**—including; **rep**—repeat

TIP

When working with a pure cotton yarn without much "give", you may find that the foundation chains are too tight to insert the hook comfortably when working the first row of stitches. When this happens, redo the chain using a size larger hook.

NOTES

1. Always read all the way through the pattern before you start and make sure that you understand the techniques involved.
2. Figures in brackets [ ] refer to the two larger sizes. Where only one figure is given this refers to all sizes.

BACK

Work 97 [107, 117] ch plus 3 turning ch.

Foundation row Insert hook into 4th ch from hook, work 1 tr in each ch to end, turn (98 [108, 118] tr, incl turning ch which counts as 1 tr).

Row 1 3 ch (counts as first htr, 1 ch), * 1 htr in next tr, miss 1 tr, 1 ch, rep from * to end of row, 1 htr into top of turning ch, turn.

Row 2 3 ch (counts as first tr), 1 tr into each htr and ch along row, ending with 1 htr into 2nd of 3 turning ch, turn (98 [108, 118] tr, incl turning ch which counts as 1 tr).

Row 3 3 ch, 1 tr into next tr, * 2 ch, miss 2 tr, 1 tr into each of next 2 tr, rep from * ending last rep 2 ch, miss 2 tr, 1 tr into last tr, 1 tr into top of turning ch, turn.

Row 4 4 ch (counts as 1 tr, 1 ch), * 2 tr into next 2 ch sp, miss 2 tr, 2 ch, rep from * to end, 1 tr into top of turning ch, turn.

Row 5 3 ch (counts as first tr), 1 tr into first 2 ch sp, * 2 ch, miss 2 tr, 2 tr into 2 ch sp, rep from * ending last rep 2 ch, miss 2 tr, 1 tr into last 2 ch sp, 1 tr into 3rd of 4 turning ch, turn.

Row 6 3 ch, 1 tr into next tr, 1 tr into each tr and ch along row, ending with 1 tr into top of turning ch, turn.

Work straight, repeating rows 1 to 6 of the pattern until you have worked 6 complete repeats in all. Work row 1 and 2, fasten off yarn.

FRONT

Work the same as for the back.

STRAPS (make 2, all sizes alike)

Work 5 ch.

Row 1 1 dc into 2nd ch from hook, 1 dc into each of next 3 ch, turn (4 dc).

Row 2 1 ch, 1 dc into each dc along row, turn (4 dc).

Row 3 1 ch, 1 dc into first dc, 2 ch, miss 2 dc, 1 dc into last dc, turn.

Row 4 1 ch, 1 dc into first dc, 2 dc into 2 ch sp, 1 dc into last dc, turn (4 dc).

Row 5 1 ch, 1 dc into each dc along row, turn.

Rep row 5 until strap measures 40.5 cm (16 in.) or desired length; finish off, leaving a long yarn end for sewing the strap to the back piece.

FINISHING

Weave in the short yarn ends, block and press each piece and allow to dry completely.

Join the front and back pieces together into a tube using the woven seam method on page 36. Work a row of double crochet edging (page 19) around the top and bottom of the tube.

Pin the ends of the straps with buttonholes to the top edge of the front, spacing them about 18 cm (7 in.) apart. Pin the other ends of the straps in a similar position on the back, tucking about 12 mm (½ in.) of the strap to the wrong side of the back. Try on the top to check the length and position of the straps and adjust as required. Using the yarn ends, stitch the strap ends securely to the wrong side of the back. Attach the buttons.

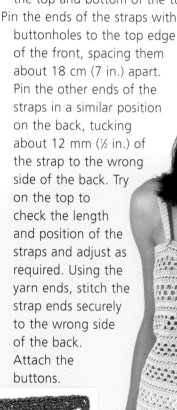

ALTERNATIVE SWATCH

This sample was worked in double strands of a fine metallic yarn to obtain a similar tension to the cotton yarn used for the model in the main photograph. See page 10 for advice on making yarn substitutions.

TEXTURED STITCHES

Any combination of stitches can be joined into a cluster by leaving the last loop of each stitch on the hook as it is made, then securing the loops together at the end. This technique is used as a method of decreasing one or more stitches (page 53) but it also makes attractive textured stitches in its own right. Puff stitches, bobbles and popcorns are all cluster variations, but they are worked using different methods.

WORKING A BASIC CLUSTER

Joining two, three or more stitches at the top as you work forms a group called a cluster. Use this technique for decorative purposes or to decrease stitches.

STEP 2 Work the last stitch of the cluster in the same way, resulting in 4 loops on the hook. Wind the yarn over the hook.

STEP 1 To work a three treble crochet cluster, yarn over hook, work the first stitch, omitting the last stage to leave 2 loops on the hook. Work the second stitch in the same way. You now have 3 loops on the hook.

STEP 3
Draw the yarn through the 4 loops on the hook to complete the cluster and secure the loops.

WORKING PUFF STITCHES

A puff stitch is a cluster of half treble crochet stitches worked in the same place – the number of stitches in each puff can vary between three and five.

STEP 1
Wrap the yarn over the hook, insert the hook into the stitch, yarn over hook again and draw a loop through (3 loops on the hook).

STEP 2
Repeat this step twice more, inserting the hook into the same stitch (7 loops on the hook).

STEP 3
Wrap the yarn over the hook and draw it through all 7 loops on the hook. Work an extra chain stitch at the top of the puff to complete the stitch.

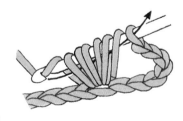

Working bobbles

A bobble is a cluster of between three and five stitches worked into the same stitch and closed at the top. Bobbles are usually worked on wrong side rows and surrounded by shorter stitches to throw them into high relief.

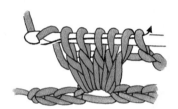

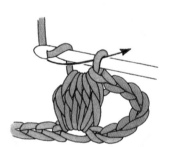

STEP 2
Work the remaining 2 stitches of the bobble in the same way, resulting in 6 loops on the hook. Wind the yarn over the hook and draw it through the 6 loops to secure them and complete the bobble. You may find it helpful to gently poke the bobble through with the tip of one finger to the other side of the work as you draw the securing loop through.

STEP 1 (wrong side)
To make a five-stitch treble crochet bobble, wrap the yarn over the hook, work the first stitch, omitting the last stage to leave 2 loops on the hook. Work the second and third stitches in the same way. You now have 4 loops on the hook.

STEP 3 (right side)
On the following row, work a row of double crochet, taking care to work one stitch into the securing stitch at the top of each bobble.

WORKING POPCORN STITCHES

A popcorn stitch is a cluster of stitches (the number may vary), which is folded and closed at the top.

STEP 1 To make a popcorn with 4 separate treble crochet stitches, work a group of 4 treble crochet stitches.

STEP 3 Pick up the working loop with the hook and draw it through to fold the group of stitches and close it at the top. The popcorn is now complete.

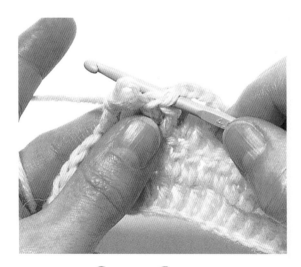

STEP 2 Take the hook out of the working loop and insert it under both loops of the first treble crochet stitch in the group.

ALTERNATIVE METHOD

A popcorn may be made from a group of separate stitches as above, or the group can share one stitch at the base like a bobble which gives a more raised effect. Popcorns worked into chain spaces are usually worked by the first method.

PROJECT 10 BOBBLE SWEATER

Two strands of yarn are worked together to create this chunky, generously sized sweater, patterned with a row of bobbles. For a tweedy effect use two colors of coordinating yarn, or if you prefer to make the sweater in a solid color, use two strands of the same shade of yarn.

SIZES

To fit sizes small/medium and medium/large, fitting loosely:

ACTUAL MEASUREMENT	. (97 [117] cm	(38 [46] in.)
SIDE LENGTH	38 [41] cm	(15 [16] in.)
SLEEVE LENGTH	48 [51] cm	(19 [20] in.)

MATERIALS

QUANTITY 13 [15] skeins of main colour (A), 13 [15] skeins of contrast colour (B); please note that one strand of each yarn is used together throughout this pattern

YARN "Shetland Jumper Weight" by Jamieson & Smith (or Shetland wool 4ply weight yarn with approx 137 m/150 yd per 1 oz skein)

COLOUR FC8 (A), 125 (B)

HOOK SIZE 4.5 mm, 5 mm, 5.5 mm (G, H, I)

NEEDLE Large tapestry needle

SPECIAL TECHNIQUES USED

Making a foundation chain (page 17)
Double crochet edging (page 37)
Working bobbles (page 100)
Increasing (pages 50–51)

CHECK YOUR TENSION

Using one strand of each yarn and the 5.5 mm (I) hook, make a foundation chain of 24 ch and work approximately 15 cm (6 in.) in pattern. Block the sample (pages 34–35), allow to dry and measure the tension (pages 44–45). The recommended tension produces 3 bobbles to 10 cm (4 in.) measured across both the stitches and the rows. (Measure from the outside edges of the outer bobbles – the whole of the outer bobbles should fit just inside the 10 cm/4 in. measurement.)

If you have more bobbles, your tension is too tight and you should make another sample using a larger hook.

If you have less bobbles, your tension is too loose and you should make another sample using a smaller hook.

ABBREVIATIONS

ch—chain; **dc**—single crochet stitch; **inc**—increase; **dec**—decrease; **st(s)** —**stitch(es)**; **WS**—wrong side; **RS**—right side

SPECIAL ABBREVIATION FOR THIS PATTERN

MB—make a four-stitch treble crochet bobble (page 100) into the next stitch

Tip

When winding yarn into a ball, ask a friend to hold the skein as you wind, or lay the skein around the back of a dining chair to prevent it from tangling. Wind the yarn loosely into a ball to avoid stretching it.

NOTES

1. Always read all the way through the pattern before you begin and make sure that you understand the techniques involved.
2. Figures in brackets [ ] refer to the larger size. Where only one figure is given it refers to both sizes.
3. Note that bobbles are made only on wrong side rows.

BACK

Using yarn A and yarn B together and the 5.5 mm (I) hook, 66 [90] ch.

Foundation row (right side) Insert hook into 2nd ch from hook, work 1 dc in each ch to end, turn. (65 [89] stitches).

Rows 1 & 2 1 ch, 1 dc into each st to end, turn.

Row 3 (wrong side) 1 ch, 1 dc into each of next 2 dc, MB in next st, * 1 dc into each of next 5 dc, MB in next st; rep from * to last 2 sts, 1 dc into each of last 2 dc, turn.

Rows 4, 5, & 6 1 ch, 1 dc into each st to end, turn.

Row 7 1 ch, 1 dc into each of next 5 dc, * MB in next st, 1 dc into each of next 5 dc; rep from * to end, turn.

Rows 8, 9, & 10 1 ch, 1 dc into each st to end, turn.

Work even in pattern, repeating rows 3–10, until you have worked 51 [56] cm (20 [22] in.), ending with a WS row. (65 [89] stitches).

SHAPE BACK NECK

Next row (right side) Work in pattern for 22 [32] sts, turn.

Continue working in pattern only on these 22 [32] sts, at the same time dec 1 st at neck edge on next 2 rows. (20 [30] stitches).

Work 2 rows straight, ending with a RS row. Fasten off yarn.

With RS facing, miss centre 21 [25] sts, rejoin yarn and work other side of back neck in pattern, reversing the shaping.

Fasten off yarn.

FRONT

Work the same as for back until the work measures 45 [50] cm (17¾ [19¾] in.), ending with WS row.

SHAPE FRONT NECK

Next row (right side) Work in pattern for 28 [38] sts, turn.

ALTERNATIVE SWATCH
Make the garment more festive by adding a fine strand of metallic thread to Shetland wool when knitting a sweater for a special occasion. Choose gold metallic to enhance warm colours such as reds, oranges and yellows, or partner cool shades of blues, lavenders and soft greens with silver metallic.

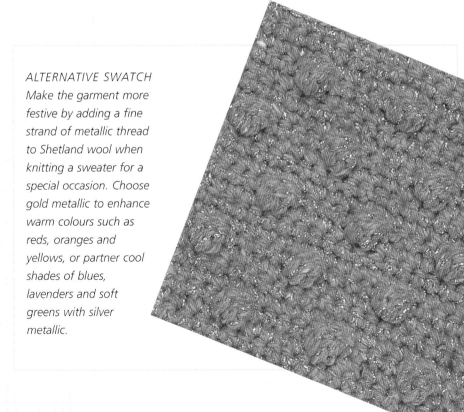

Continue working in pattern only on these 28 [38] sts, at the same time dec 1 st at neck edge on every row until 20 [30] sts remain.

Work straight in pattern until back measures the same as the front, ending with a RS row. (20 [30] stitches).

With RS facing, miss centre 9 [13] sts, rejoin yarn and work other side of front neck in pattern, reversing the shaping.

Fasten off yarn.

SLEEVES (MAKE 2)

Using yarn A and yarn B together and the 5.5 mm (I) hook, 38 [48] ch.

Foundation row (right side) Insert hook into 2nd ch from hook, work 1 dc in each ch to end, turn. (37 [47] stitches).

Work in pattern as for back, at the same time inc 1st at each end of every 5th row until there are 59 [69] stitches.

Work straight in pattern until work measures 44.5 [47] cm (17½ [18½] in.), ending with a WS row on which bobbles have been made.

Work 3 more rows of double crochet.

Fasten off yarn.

FINISHING

Weave in the short yarn ends, block each piece and allow to dry completely.

With right sides together, join the front and back together at the shoulders, using one of the methods shown on page 36.

Measure the top of the sleeves and mark the centre point with a pin. With right sides together, join the sleeves to the front and back, aligning the centre points with the shoulder seams.

With right sides together, join the sleeve and side seams.

WORKING THE EDGING

Neck Using yarn A and yarn B together and with the RS of the work facing, rejoin yarn to neck edge at shoulder seam. Using the 5 mm (H) hook, work a row of evenly spaced double crochet edging (page 37) around the neck and join with sl st to first dc. Change to the 4.5 mm (G) hook

and work two more rows of double crochet, joining each row with with sl st to first dc.

Fasten off yarn.

Cuffs Using yarn A and yarn B together and with the RS of the work facing, rejoin yarn to cuff at sleeve seam. Using the 4.5 mm (G) hook, work two rows of evenly spaced double crochet edging (page 37) around the cuff, joining each row with with sl st to first dc.

Fasten off yarn.

Hem Using yarn A and yarn B together and with the RS of the work facing, rejoin yarn to hem at side seam. Using the 5 mm (H) hook, work a row of evenly spaced double crochet edging (page 37) around the hem and join with sl st to first dc. Change to the 4.5 mm (G) hook and work one more row of double crochet, join with sl st to first dc.

Fasten off yarn and weave in all remaining yarn ends.

Braids, edgings, borders

Braids, edgings and borders are strips of crochet which can be stitched to pieces of crochet or woven fabrics to decorate the edges. Depending on the pattern, they can be worked in short rows across the width or in long rows across the length.

Braids are narrow, both edges are usually shaped rather than straight, and some braid patterns such as Chain Braid (page 107) may be worked in more than one colour of yarn. When made from fine cotton, cotton blend or metallic yarns using a small hook, the effect is similar to the ready-made braids used to decorate home furnishings such as lampshades, cushions, and fabric-covered boxes and baskets. Hand-stitch a braid to fabric using tiny stitches down the centre or along each edge with matching sewing thread. Providing the glue is compatible with the fibre composition of the yarn, use a glue gun to attach braid to a box or basket.

Edgings and borders usually have one straight and one shaped edge and look similar to each other. One exception to this rule is Faux Ribbing (page 108), which is a straight-edged, slightly stretchy strip which makes a good band for cuffs and hems of garments, simulating knitted ribbing. As a general rule, edgings are narrower in width than borders and the patterns are less complex.

WORKING A SINGLE COLOUR BRAID

Many braids are worked widthways on a small number of stitches. Keep turning the braid and repeating the pattern row until it is the required length, then fasten off the yarn.

WORKING A TWO COLOUR BRAID

Fancy braid patterns, worked in two or more colours, usually have a foundation made by working widthways, then extra rows of crochet are worked along the two long edges. The extra rows can be worked in contrasting yarn colours or in a metallic yarn of the same weight.

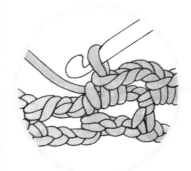

Braids pattern library

Interwoven braid

Foundation ring 7 ch and join with sl st to form a ring.

Foundation row 3 ch, 3 tr into ring, 3 ch, 1 dc into ring, turn.

Row 1 3 ch, 3 tr into 3 ch sp, 3 ch, 1 dc into same 3 ch sp, turn.

Rep row 1.

Chain braid

Foundation chain Using yarn A, 3 ch.

Braid foundation 1 dtr into 4th ch from hook, turn, * 4 ch, 1 dtr into sp between dtr and ch, turn; rep from * for length required. Fasten off yarn A.

Row 1 (worked into one edge of base) Using yarn B, * 2 dc into sp between dtr and ch, 3 ch; rep from * to end, ending with 2 dc. Fasten off yarn B.

Row 2 (worked into remaining edge of base) Using yarn C, rep row 1.

Fasten off yarn C.

Looped braid

Foundation chain Using yarn A, 6 ch.

Braid foundation 1 tr into 5th ch from hook, 1 dc into last ch, turn, * 4 ch, 1 tr into dc, 1 dc into tr, turn; rep from * for length required.

Fasten off yarn A.

Row 1 (worked into one edge of base) Using yarn B, 1 dc into first dc, * 5 ch, 1 tr into side of next dc; rep from * to end.

Row 2 (worked into remaining edge of base) Rep row 1.

Fasten off yarn B.

Picot braid

Foundation chain 4 ch.

Braid foundation 1 tr into 4th ch from hook, turn, * 4 ch, 1 dtr into sp between dtr and ch, turn; rep from * for length required.

Row 1 (worked into one edge of base) [2 dc, 3 ch, 2 dc] into first sp at end of braid, * [2 dc, 3 ch, 2 dc] into next sp; rep from * to end. Break off yarn.

Row 2 (worked into remaining edge of base) Rejoin yarn, rep row 1.

Fasten off yarn.

STEP 1

To make sure the finished edging or border is the correct length when a pattern is worked lengthways, make an approximate foundation chain about 25 stitches longer than the pattern states. Work the first pattern row along the chain in the usual way, checking the length of your work against the edge you wish to decorate. When crochet and edge match in length (and you have the correct multiple of stitches to work the pattern), turn and work the second row, leaving the extra chains unworked.

STEP 2

When the edging or border is complete, snip off the slip knot at the end of the chain with a sharp pair of scissors. Using a tapestry needle, unpick the first one or two chain stitches until the chains will slip through each other when the yarn end is pulled. Unravel the chain up to the edge of the crochet, then weave the yarn end in the usual way.

EDGINGS AND BORDERS PATTERN LIBRARY

FAUX RIBBING

Worked widthways.
Foundation chain Work the number of chains to suit the width of ribbing you require.
Foundation row 1 dc into 2nd ch from hook, 1 dc into each ch to end, turn.
Row 1 1 ch, work 1 dc into back loop of each st along row, turn. Rep row 1.

CHAIN LOOP BORDER

Worked lengthways.

Foundation chain Make the required length of foundation chain.

Row 1 1 dc into 2nd ch from hook, 1 dc into each ch to end, turn.

Row 2 1 ch, 1 dc into each dc to end, turn.

Row 3 1 ch, 1 dc into first dc, * 1 dc into next st, 15 ch, sl st into same place as dc just worked; rep from * to end.

Fasten off yarn.

SHELL BORDER

Worked lengthways.

The foundation chain for this pattern requires a multiple of 10 stitches plus 3. Make the required length of foundation chain.

Row 1 (right side) 1 tr into 4th ch from hook, 1 tr into each ch to end, turn.

Row 2 1 ch, 1 dc into each of first 3 tr, * 2 ch, miss 2 tr, [2 tr, 2 ch] twice into next tr, miss 2 tr, 1 dc into each of next 5 tr; rep from * to end omitting 2 dc at end of last rep and working last dc into top of 3 ch at beg of

NARROW LOOPED EDGING

Worked lengthways.

The foundation chain for this pattern requires a multiple of 4 stitches plus 2. Make the required length of foundation chain.

Row 1 (right side) 1 dc into 2nd ch from hook, 1 dc into each ch to end, turn.

Row 2 1 ch, 1 dc into first dc, * 5 ch, miss 3 dc, 1 dc into next dc; rep from * to end.

Row 3 1 ch, 1 dc into first dc, * 7 ch, 1 dc into next dc; rep from * to end.

Fasten off yarn.

previous row, turn.

Row 3 1 ch, 1 dc into each of first 2 dc, * 3 ch, miss next 2 ch sp, [3 tr, 2 ch, 3 tr] into next 2 ch sp, 3 ch, miss 1 dc, 1 dc into next 3 dc; rep from * to end omitting 1 dc at end of last rep, turn.

Row 4 1 ch, 1 dc into first dc, * 4 ch, miss next 3 ch sp, [4 tr, 2 ch, 4 tr] into next 2 ch sp, 4 ch, miss 1 dc, 1 dc into next dc; rep from * to end, turn.

Row 5 1 ch, 1 dc into first dc, * 5 ch, skip next 4 ch sp, [4 tr, 2 ch, 4 tr] into next 2 ch sp, 5 ch, 1 dc into next dc; rep from * to end.

Fasten off yarn.

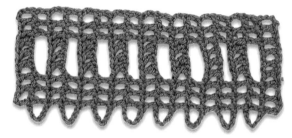

POINTED BORDER

Worked widthways.

Foundation chain 20 ch, turn.

Foundation row 1 tr into 6th ch from hook, * 1 ch, miss 1 ch, 1 tr into next ch; rep from * to end, turn.

Row 1 (right side) 7 ch; 1 tr into first tr, [1 ch, 1 tr into next tr] twice, 7 ch, miss 3 tr, [1 tr into next tr, 1 ch] twice, miss 1 ch, 1 tr into next ch, turn.

Row 2 4 ch (counts as 1 tr, 1 ch), miss first tr, 1 tr into next tr, 1 ch, 1 tr into next tr, [1 ch, miss 1 ch, 1 tr into next ch] 3 times, [1 ch, 1 tr into next tr] 3 times.

Rep rows 1 and 2.

WORKING A HEADING

Many edgings and borders benefit from the addition of a heading (two or more rows of plain double crochet worked to strengthen the straight edge) when trimming household items such as towels, bed and table linen which will be laundered frequently.

WORKING AN EDGING OR BORDER LENGTHWISE

Working a heading as an integral part of an edging or border worked lengthways is a simple matter of working an extra two or more rows of double crochet between the foundation chain and the stitch pattern.

WORKING AN EDGING OR BORDER WIDTHWISE

To work a heading on to an edging or border worked widthways, first work complete pattern. Rejoin the same yarn at the right-hand corner of the straight edge (with right side facing you and the straight edge at the top) and work an evenly spaced row of double crochet stitches into the edge. Work two or more rows of double crochet to complete the heading.

APPLYING A CROCHET EDGING TO A PIECE OF CROCHET

Pin the edging or border to the crochet fabric with right sides facing and straight edges aligning. Using matching yarn, threaded in a large tapestry needle, overcast together, taking the needle through the crochet edge and both loops of the edging or border.

APPLYING A CROCHET EDGING TO A FABRIC EDGE

Pin the edging or border to the hemmed fabric edge with right sides facing and straight edges aligning. Using a matching sewing thread or embroidery floss (depending on the weight of both crochet and fabric) threaded in a sewing needle, overcast together, taking the needle through the fabric edge and both loops of the edging or border.

APPLYING A CROCHET EDGING TO A FLAT PIECE OF FABRIC

Pin the edging or border to the fabric with the right sides of both crochet and fabric facing upwards. Using a matching sewing thread or stranded embroidery cotton (depending on the weight of both crochet and fabric) threaded in a sewing needle, stitch together with small, neat stitches, taking the needle through both loops of the edging or border and then into the fabric.

PROJECT 11
EDWARDIAN BORDERED TOWELS

Beautiful lace edgings decorate a quartet of guest towels to add style to the period bathroom. Work longer lengths of the edgings and add them to the edges of larger towels, or work them in a finer yarn to decorate bed linen.

SIZES

Shell and Lattice Edging – 4 cm (1½ in.) deep
Arch Edging – 5 cm (2 in.) deep
Vandyke Petal Edging – 10 cm (4 in.) deep
Fence Edging – 10 cm (4 in.) deep
The edgings can be made to any length

MATERIALS

QUANTITY 1 x 50 g ball of A, 2 x 50 g balls of B
YARN "Cotton Glace" by Rowan (or pure cotton lightweight DK yarn with approx 114 m/125 yd per 50 g ball)
COLOUR 726 Bleached (A), 725 Ecru (B)
HOOK SIZE 2.5 mm, 3 mm (B, C)
NEEDLE Sewing needle
Four guest towels approx 38 cm (15 in.) wide
Matching sewing thread
Pins

SPECIAL TECHNIQUES USED

Working a foundation chain (*page 16*)
Working an edging widthwise (*page 110*)
Working an edging lengthwise (*page 110*)
Attaching an edging to fabric (*page 106*)

CHECK YOUR TENSION

Work about 15 cm (6 in.) of each edging pattern. Block (page 34) and press the sample, allow to dry and measure the tension (page 44). The recommended tension for each pattern is:
    Shell and Lattice Edging – 2 pattern repeats to 5 cm (2 in.)
    Arch Edging – 2 pattern repeats to 9 cm (3½ in.)
    Vandyke Petal Edging – 2 pattern repeats to 4 cm (1½ in.)
    Fence Edging—2 pattern repeats to 8 cm (3 in.)
    If you have a smaller pattern repeat, your tension is too tight and you should make another sample using a larger hook.
    If you have a larger pattern repeat, your tension is too loose and you should make another sample using a smaller hook.

ABBREVIATIONS

sl st—slip-stitch; **ch**—chain; **dc**—double crochet; **tr**—treble crochet; **sp**—space; **st(s)**—stitch(es), **incl**—including; **rep**—repeat

TIP

Each of the designs features a plain double crochet heading along the top edge of the lace, either worked as an integral part of the pattern or added at the end. The heading gives a stable, hard-wearing edge which is perfect for attaching to items of home furnishings such as towels and bed linen which will be laundered frequently.

NOTES

1. Always read all the way through the pattern before you begin and make sure that you understand the techniques involved.
2. Shell and Lattice Edging and Arch Edging are worked with an integral heading. The headings on the other two edgings are added after the edgings are finished.
3. Shell and Lattice Edging and Arch Edging are worked lengthways; Vandyke Petal Edging and Fence Edging are worked widthways.

Shell and lattice edging

Fence edging

Arch edging

Vandyke petal edging

WORKING SHELL AND LATTICE EDGING

Using yarn A and the 3 mm (C) hook, work a foundation chain containing a multiple of 6 sts plus 3 – the chain should be about 2.5 cm (1 in.) longer than the towel edge. Change to the 2.5 mm (B) hook to work the edging.

Row 1 (right side) Work 1 dc into 2nd ch from hook, 1 dc into each ch to end, turn.

Row 2, 3 & 4 1 ch, 1 dc into each dc to end, turn.

Row 5 3 ch (counts as 1 tr), miss first dc, 1 tr into next dc, * 1 ch, miss 1 dc, 1 tr into each of next 2 dc; rep from * to end, turn.

Row 6 5 ch (counts as 1 tr, 2 ch), 1 dc into next 1 ch sp, * 4 ch, 1 dc into next 1 ch sp; rep from * to last 2 sts, 2 ch, 1 tr into 3rd of 3 ch, turn.

Row 7 1 ch, 1 dc into first tr, * work 7 tr into next 4 ch sp, 1 dc into next 4 ch sp; rep from * to end, placing last dc into 3rd of 5 ch.
Fasten off yarn.

WORKING ARCH EDGING

Using yarn A and the 3 mm (C) hook, work a foundation chain containing a multiple of 10 sts plus 2 – the chain should be about 2.5 cm (1 in.) longer than the towel edge. Change to the 2.5 mm (B) hook to work the edging.

Row 1 (right side) Work 1 dc into 2nd ch from hook, 1 dc into each ch to end, turn.

Rows 2 & 3 1 ch, 1 dc into each dc to end, turn.

Row 4 3 ch (counts as 1 tr), miss first dc, 1 tr into each of next 3 dc, * 1 ch, miss 1 dc, 1 tr into next dc, 1 ch, miss 1 dc, 1 tr into each of next 7 dc; rep from * to end omitting 3 tr at end of last rep, turn.

Row 5 1 ch, 1 dc into each of first 4 tr, 2 dc into each of next two 1 ch sp, * 1 dc into each of next 7 tr, 2 dc into each of next 2 ch sp; rep from * to last 4 tr, 1 dc into each of next 3 tr, 1 dc into 3rd of 3 ch, turn.

Row 6 1 ch, 1 dc into first dc, 2 ch, miss 2 dc, 1 dc into next dc, 8 ch, miss 4 dc, 1 dc into next dc, * 5 ch, miss 5 dc, 1 dc into next dc, 8 ch, miss 4 dc, 1 dc into next dc; rep from * to last 3 dc, 2 ch, 1 dc into last dc, turn.

Row 7 1 ch, 1 dc into first dc, 19 tr into 8 ch arch, * 1 dc into next 5 ch sp, 19 tr into next 8 ch arch; rep from * to last 2 ch sp, 1 dc into last dc.
Fasten off yarn.

Working Vandyke Petal Edging

Using yarn B and the 2.5 mm (B) hook, work a foundation chain of 23 ch.

Row 1 (wrong side) Work 1 tr into 8th ch from hook, miss 2 ch, [1 tr, 2 ch, 1 tr] into next ch, miss 2 ch , 1 tr into next ch, 2 ch, miss 2 ch, 1 tr into next ch, 5 ch, miss 5 ch, [1 tr, 3 ch, 1 tr] into last ch, turn.

Row 2 (right side) 3 ch (counts as 1 tr), 7 tr into 3 ch loop, 1 tr into next tr, 7 tr into 5 ch sp, 1 tr into next tr, 2 ch, miss 2 ch, 1 tr into next tr, [1 tr, 2 ch, 1 tr] into next sp, miss 1 tr, 1 tr into next tr, 2 ch, miss 2 ch, 1 tr into next ch, turn.

Row 3 5 ch, 1 tr into first tr, [1 tr, 2 ch, 1 tr] into next sp, miss 1 tr, 1 tr into next tr, 2 ch, miss 2 ch, 1 tr into next tr, 5 ch, miss 7 tr, [1 tr, 3 ch, 1 tr] into next tr, turn.

Repeat rows 2 and 3 until edging is desired length, ending repeat with row 2.

Fasten off yarn.

Working the Heading

With RS facing, rejoin the yarn to the top right-hand corner of the edging.

Next row (right side) 1 ch, work dc into the loops along the top of the edging, working 3 dc into the first loop, 2 dc into the second loop and rep along the row, turn.

Next 2 rows 1 ch, 1 dc into each dc along row.

Fasten off yarn.

Working Fence Edging

Using yarn B and the 2.5 mm (B) hook, work a foundation chain of 20 ch.

Row 1 (right side) Work 1 tr into 7th ch from hook, [1 ch, miss 1 ch, 1 tr into next ch] twice, 2 tr into each of next 2 ch, [1 tr into next ch, 1 ch, miss 1 ch] 3 times, 1 tr into last st, turn.

Row 2 7 ch, 1 tr into first 1 ch sp, [1 ch, 1 tr into next 1 ch sp] twice, 4 ch, [1 tr into next 1 ch sp, 1 ch] twice, 1 tr into top of turning ch, 1 tr into next ch, turn.

Row 3 4 ch, [1 tr into next 1 ch sp, 1 ch] twice, 6 tr into 4 ch loop, [1 ch, 1 tr into next 1 ch sp] twice, 1 ch, 12 tr into 7 ch loop at end of row and secure with sl st into last st of foundation ch, turn.

Row 4 5 ch, 1 dc into 2nd st, [5 ch, miss 1 st, 1 dc into next st] 5 times, 1 ch, [1 tr into next 1 ch sp, 1 ch] twice, 1 tr into next 1 ch sp, 4 ch, [1 tr into next 1 ch sp, 1 ch] twice, 1 tr into first st of turning ch, 1 tr into next st, turn.

Row 5 4 ch, [1 tr into next 1 ch sp, 1 ch] twice, 6 tr into 4 ch loop, 1 ch, [1 tr into next 1 ch sp, 1 ch] twice, 1 tr into first ch of 5 ch, turn.

Row 6 7 ch, 1 tr into first ch sp, [1 ch, 1 tr into next 1 ch sp] twice, 4 ch, [1 tr into next 1 ch sp, 1 ch] twice, 1 tr into top of turning ch, 1 tr into next ch, turn.

Row 7 4 ch, [1 tr into next 1 ch sp, 1 ch] twice, 6 tr into 4 ch loop, [1 ch, 1 tr into next 1 ch sp] twice, 1 ch, 12 tr into 7 ch loop at end of row and secure with sl st into first ch of 5 ch close to the tr previously worked, turn.

Row 8 5 ch, 1 dc into 2nd st, [5 ch, miss 1 st, 1 dc into next st] 5 times, 1 ch, [1 tr into next 1 ch sp, 1 ch] twice, 1 tr into next 1 ch sp, 4 ch, [1 tr into next 1 ch sp, 1 ch] twice, 1 tr into first st of turning ch, 1 tr into next st, turn.

Repeat rows 5 to 8 until edging is desired length, ending repeat with row 7.

Fasten off yarn.

Working the Heading

With RS facing, rejoin the yarn to the top right-hand corner of the edging.

Next row (right side) 1 ch, work an evenly spaced row of dc into the loops along the top of the edging, working 2 dc into the first loop, 3 dc into the second loop and rep along the row, turn.

Next 2 rows 1 ch, 1 dc into each dc along row.

Fasten off yarn.

Finishing

Weave in the short yarn ends, block and press (page 34) each piece, and allow to dry completely.

Pin the edgings evenly onto the towels. Using sewing thread to match the yarn colour and a sewing needle, sew the edgings onto the towels along the tops (page 111).

THE PERSONAL TOUCH

Buttons, cords, spirals and fringes can add your very own touch to crochet items. Crochet buttons are fun to make, whether ball buttons or flat ring buttons, and they can be made to match or contrast in colour with a garment or cushion cover. Crochet cords make straps for bags, ties to secure a neckline, or several lengths can be sewn on to a plain piece of crochet to decorate it with shapes such as spirals, stripes or swirls. Use a crochet spiral to trim a key ring or the tab on a zip. You can make a cluster of them to decorate each corner of an afghan as a novel alternative to a tassel. A simple tasselled fringe is a favourite finishing touch for a scarf, shawl or wrap.

STEP 2 Slip the bead or ball into the cover. Start decreasing (page 53) by working * 1 dc into next st, dc2tog; repeat from * until the bead or ball is completely covered.

MAKING A BALL BUTTON

STEP 1 Work a ball button over a bead or a small ball of stuffing. Using a smaller hook than suggested for the yarn you are using, 2 ch, then work 4 dc into the first ch. Without joining or turning the work, work 2 dc into each stitch (page 50) made on the previous round. For the next and every following increase round, work * 1 dc in first st, 2 dc into next stitch; repeat from * until the piece covers one half of the bead or ball of stuffing.

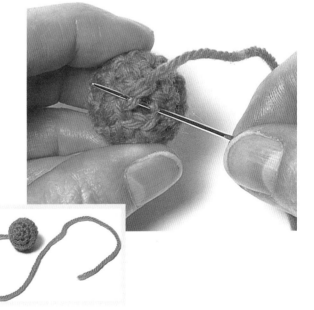

STEP 3 Break off the yarn, leaving an end of about 30 cm (12 in.). Thread the yarn into a large tapestry needle and work a few stitches to secure. Don't cut the yarn, instead use it to attach the button to the garment.

MAKING A RING BUTTON

STEP 1 Work a ring button over a
plastic ring – choose a ring which is slightly
smaller than the size you require for the
finished button. Starting with a slip knot
on the hook, work a round of double
crochet stitches over the ring until it is
completely covered.

STEP 2 Join with a slipstitch to the first stitch. Break off
the yarn, leaving an end of about 30 cm (12 in.) and thread it
into a large tapestry needle. Sew a row of running stitches
around the edge of the crochet. Turning the edge of the
crochet to the centre of the ring, draw the thread up firmly
and secure it.

STEP 3 On the back
of the button, work strands
of yarn diagonally across the
button several times to
make a shank. Sew the
button on to the garment
by sewing through the
centre of the strands.

CROCHET CORDS IN THREE WIDTHS

Above—Single slip stitch cord
Middle—Double slip stitch cord
Below—Double crochet cord

MAKING A SINGLE SLIPSTITCH CORD

Work a foundation chain to the required length (see page 108 for how to make an approximate foundation chain). Change to a size smaller hook, insert into the second chain from the hook and work a row of slipstitch (page 19) along one side of the chain.

MAKING A DOUBLE SLIPSTITCH CORD

Work a foundation chain to the required length (see page 108 for how to make an approximate foundation chain). Change to a size smaller hook, insert into the second chain from the hook and work a row of slipstitch (page 19) along each side of the chain, turning with 1 ch at the end of the first side.

MAKING A DOUBLE CROCHET CORD

STEP 1 Work a foundation chain to the required length (see page 108 for how to make an approximate foundation chain). Change to a size smaller hook, insert into the second chain from the hook and work a row of double crochet stitches (pages 19–20) along one side of the chain.

STEP 2 At the end of the first side, 1 ch, turn, and work along the second side of the chain in the same way.

MAKING A PLAIN SPIRAL

STEP 1 Work a loose foundation chain of 30 stitches. Change to a size smaller hook and work two treble crochet stitches into the fourth chain from the hook. Continue along the chain working four treble crochet stitches into each chain.

STEP 2
As you work, the crochet will begin to twist into a spiral formation naturally. Fasten off the yarn at the end of the row, leaving a yarn end of about 30 cm (12 in.) to attach the spiral.

MAKING A STRIPED SPIRAL

Using yarn A, work a plain spiral as above, leaving a long yarn end for attaching the finished spiral. Join yarn B to the outer edge of the top of the spiral and work a row of double crochet stitches along the edge. Fasten off the ends of yarn B.

PLAIN AND STRIPED SPIRALS
Above—Plain spiral
Below—Striped spiral

Making a fringe tassel

STEP 1 Decide how
deep the finished fringe will
be and cut a rectangle of
stiff cardboard to the same
depth plus 1 cm (½ in.) to
allow for trimming. Wind
yarn evenly around the
cardboard and cut along the
bottom edge to make
strands. Repeat until you
have the required number
of strands.

STEP 2 Mark the
position of each fringe tassel
on the right side of the
crochet edge with pins. Insert
a large hook from front to
back through the crochet.
Gather the required number
of yarn strands into a neat
group, fold in half and loop
the fold over the hook.

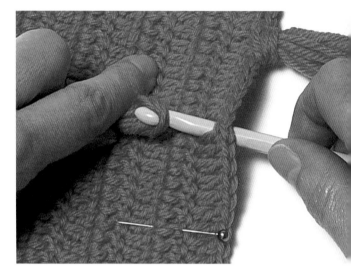

STEP 3 Carefully pull
the hook and the folded yarn
strands through the crochet
for a short distance.

STEP 4 Loop the hook
around the cut ends of the
yarn group and pull gently
through to complete the
tassel. Repeat until the fringe
is complete, then carefully
trim the cut ends with a
sharp pair of scissors.

PROJECT 12 WINTER JACKET

This loosely fitting, boxy jacket is worked in a range of glowing jewel colours using a wonderfully soft yarn made from the finest Merino wool. The interlocking striped pattern consists of two stitches of different heights and is deceptively easy to work.

SIZES

One size to fit bust/chest 91–97 cm (36–38 in.)

ACTUAL MEASUREMENT 107 cm (42 in.)

SIDE LENGTH 36 cm (14 in.) including edging

SLEEVE LENGTH (measured straight from top of sleeve to cuff edge) 46 cm (18 in.)

MATERIALS

QUANTITY 6 x 50 g balls of A, 3 x balls of B, 2 x balls of C, 3 x balls of D, 2 x balls of E, 3 x balls of F, 2 x balls of G

YARN "Extra Fine Merino" Double Knitting by Jaeger (or pure wool DK yarn with approx 125 m/137 yd per 50 g ball)

COLOUR 943 Raspberry (A), 944 Elderberry (B), 979 Tango (C), 984 Violet (D), 971 Loden (E), 920 Wineberry (F), 923 Satinwood (G)

HOOK SIZE 3.5 mm, 4 mm, 4.5 mm (E, F, G)

NEEDLE Large tapestry needle

7 beads to make buttons

SPECIAL TECHNIQUES USED

Making a foundation chain (page 17)

Increasing (pages 50–51)

Double crochet edging (page 37)

Making button loops (page 41)

Making crochet buttons (pages 116–117)

CHECK YOUR TENSION

Make a foundation chain of 37 ch and work approximately 15 cm (6 in.) in pattern. Block the sample (pages 34–35), allow to dry and measure the tension (pages 44–45). The recommended tension is 20 stitches and 10 rows to 10 cm (4 in.).

If you have more stitches and rows, your tension is too tight and you should make another sample using a larger hook.

If you have less stitches and rows, your tension is too loose and you should make another sample using a smaller hook.

ABBREVIATIONS

ch—chain; **dc**—double crochet; **tr**—treble crochet; **inc**—increase; **st**(**s**)—stitch(es)

Tip

If you don't want to make your own crochet buttons, choose ready-made ones in wood or metal, preferably ones with a shank so the buttons will sit better in the loops.

NOTES

1. Always read all the way through the pattern before you begin and make sure that you understand the techniques involved.
2. Page 18 has more information about the appropriate turning chains for double and treble crochet stitches.

Colour sequence for back and front

Work two-row stripes of pattern in the following colour sequence:

1 Raspberry	2 Elderberry	3 Raspberry
4 Tango	5 Violet	6 Raspberry
7 Loden	8 Violet	9 Wineberry
10 Elderberry	11 Satinwood	12 Wineberry
13 Violet	14 Elderberry	15 Raspberry
16 Tango	17 Raspberry	18 Loden
19 Violet	20 Satinwood	21 Wineberry
22 Elderberry	23 Wineberry	24 Violet
25 Tango	26 Raspberry	27 Loden
28 Raspberry	29 Satinwood	30 Raspberry
31 Elderberry	32 Violet	33 Wineberry
34 Elderberry	35 Tango	36 Loden
37 Raspberry.		

Back

Using yarn A (Raspberry) and the 4.5 mm (G) hook, 109 ch. Change to the 4 mm (F) hook.

Row 1 (right side) Insert hook into 3rd ch from hook (counts as 1 dc), 1 dc into each of next 3 ch, * 1 tr into each of next 4 ch, 1 dc into each of next 4 ch; rep from * to end, turn.

Row 2 1 ch, 1 dc into each of next 4 sts, * 1 tr into each of next 4 sts, 1 dc into each of next 4 sts; rep from * to end, turn. Break off yarn A.

Row 3 Join in yarn B (Elderberry), 3 ch (counts as 1 tr), miss first st, 1 tr into each of next 3 sts, * 1 dc into each of next 4 sts, 1 tr into each of next 4 sts; rep from * to end, working last tr into top of turning chain.

Row 4 Rep row 3. Break off yarn B.

Rows 5 & 6 Join in yarn A (Raspberry), rep row 2. Work straight in pattern, repeating rows 3, 4, 5 and 6, changing the yarn colour after every two rows as given in the colour sequence, above, ending by working one extra row in yarn A. Fasten off yarn.

Front (make 2)

Using yarn A (Raspberry) and the 4.5 mm (G) hook, 53 ch. Change to the 4 mm (F) hook.

Work in pattern exactly as for the back, changing the yarn colour after every two rows as given in the colour sequence, above, ending by working one extra row in yarn A (Raspberry).

Colour sequence for sleeves

Work two-row stripes of pattern in the same colour sequence as the back and fronts, omitting stripes 1–5 and beginning with stripe 6, in yarn A (Raspberry).

Sleeves (make 2)

Using yarn A and the 4.5 mm (G) hook, 45 ch. Change to the 4 mm (F) hook.

Work in pattern exactly as for the back, changing the yarn colour after every two rows as given in the colour sequence, above, and ending by working one extra row in yarn A (Raspberry). At the same time, increase 1 st at each end of every 3rd row until there are 76 sts.

Work straight in pattern until the colour sequence is complete, then work one extra row in yarn A (Raspberry).

Fasten off yarn.

Finishing

Weave in the short yarn ends, block each piece and allow to dry completely.

When dealing with the ends on the right front, weave them in on the right side for the top 19 cm (7½ in.) as the top of the right front will be turned back to form the collar, leaving the wrong side of the work visible. Weave in the ends as usual on the wrong side as here the joins occur on the armhole edge, not on the front edge.

With right sides together, join the fronts and back together at the shoulders, leaving the centre 18 cm (7 in.) open, using one of the methods shown on page 36.

Measure the top of the sleeves and mark the centre point with a pin. With right sides facing, join the sleeves to the fronts and back aligning the centre points with the shoulder seams.

With right sides togther, join the sleeve and side seams.

Working the edging

Row 1 With right side facing, join yarn A (Raspberry) to the lower edge of the jacket. Using the 3.5 mm (E) hook, work one row of evenly spaced double crochet edging (page 37) along the lower edge, front edges, and neck, working 1 ch at corners, 2 dc into sts at either side of shoulder seams. Along front edges of left and right fronts, space stitches evenly by working 2 dc into each tr row end, 1 dc into each dc row end. Join with sl st into first dc.

Row 2 1 ch, work 1 dc into each dc in previous row, working 3 dc into ch sp at each corner and making 7 button loops along the right front as follows: 3 dc into 1 ch sp at bottom corner of right front, 1 dc into next dc, * miss 2 dc, 4 ch, 1 dc into each of next 10 dc; rep from * 6 times, continue as established in dc. Join with sl st into first dc.

Row 3 1 ch, work 1 dc into each dc in previous row, working 3 dc into 2nd stitch of 3 dc group at each corner and [3 dc, 3 ch, 3 dc] into each 4 ch button loop along right front. Join with sl st into first dc.

Fasten off yarn.

Making the buttons

Using yarn A (Raspberry) and a small hook, make 7 ball buttons following the instructions on page 116. Stitch securely in place on the left front to correspond with the button loops. Weave in the remaining yarn ends. Fold back 19 cm (7½ in.) of left and right fronts to make collar and press the fold very lightly with a warm, dry iron.

ALTERNATIVE SWATCH
The interlocking pattern looks just as effective worked with a smaller number of colours. Here, light and dark shades of the same colour worked in alternate two-row stripes show the pattern well.

GLOSSARY

Ball band—The paper strip around a ball of yarn giving information about weight, shade number, batch number, fibre content, and care instructions. A ball band may also contain other details including yardage and suggested tension.

Batch number—The batch of dye used for a specific ball of yarn. Shades can vary between batches, so use yarn from the same batch to make an item.

Blocking—Setting a piece of crochet by stretching and pinning it out on a flat surface before steaming or treating with cold water.

Border—A deep, decorative strip of crochet usually worked with one straight and one shaped edge which is used for trimming pieces of crochet or fabric.

Braid—A narrow, decorative strip of crochet similar in appearance to a purchased furnishing braid.

Decrease—To reduce the number of working stitches.

Edge finish—A decorative crochet edging worked directly into a crochet edge.

Edging—A narrow strip of crochet usually with one straight and one shaped edge used for trimming pieces of crochet or fabric.

Fibre—Naturally occurring or man-made substances spun together to make yarn.

Filet crochet—A type of patterned crochet where the pattern elements are worked solidly and set against a regularly worked mesh background. Filet crochet is usually worked from a chart.

Foundation chain—A length of chain stitches that forms the base row for a piece of crochet.

Foundation row—In a stitch pattern, the first row worked after the foundation chain that is not repeated as part of the pattern.

Heading—Extra rows of plain crochet worked on the long straight edge of an edging or border to add strength and durability.

Increase—To make the number of working stitches larger.

Medallion—See Motif.

Motif—A shaped piece of crochet, often worked in rounds, which can be joined together rather like fabric patchwork to make a larger piece. May also be known as a medallion.

Pattern—A set of instructions showing how to make a garment or other crochet item.

Pattern repeat—The specific number of rows or rounds that are needed to complete one stitch pattern.

Picot—A decorative chain loop, often closed into a ring with a slip stitch. The number of chains in a picot can vary.

Ply—The number of strands that are twisted together to make a yarn.

Right side—The front of crochet fabric. This side is usually visible on a finished item.

Round—A row of crochet worked in the round. Rounds are usually worked without turning so that the right side of the work is always facing the worker and the end of one round is joined to the beginning of the same round.

Row—A line of stitches worked from side to side of a flat piece of crochet.

Seam—The join made where two pieces of crochet are stitched or crocheted together.

Sewing needle—A needle with a sharp point used for applying a crochet braid, edging or border to a piece of fabric.

Starting chain—A specific number of chain stitches worked at the beginning of a round to bring the hook up to the correct height for the next stitch that is being worked.

Stitch pattern—A sequence or combination of stitches that is repeated over and over again to create a crochet fabric.

Tapestry needle—A blunt-pointed embroidery needle used for sewing pieces of crochet together.

Tension—The looseness or tightness of a crochet fabric expressed as a specific number of rows and stitches in a given area, usually 10 cm (4 in.) square.

Turning chain—A specific number of chain stitches worked at the beginning of a row to bring the hook up to the correct height for the next stitch that is being worked.

Wrong side—The reverse side of crochet fabric. This side is not usually visible on a finished item.

INDEX

WEB RESOURCES

A comprehensive selection of European and American crochet hooks are available from:
www.karpstyles.ca

European aluminium and bamboo crochet hooks are available from:
www.kgctrading.co.uk

Jaeger yarns are available from:
www.ethknits.co.uk
www.buy-mail.co.uk
www.colourway.co.uk
www.mcadirect.com
www.upcountry.co.uk

Jamieson & Smith yarns are available by worldwide mail order from:
www.shetland-wool-brokers.zetnet.co.uk

Rowan yarns are available from:
www.buy-mail.co.uk
www.colourway.co.uk
www.mcadirect.com
www.upcountry.co.uk
Rowan have a list of UK stockists on their site at
www.knitrowan.com

Sirdar yarns are available from:
www.ethknits.co.uk
www.knitwellwools.co.uk
Sirdar have a list of UK stockists on their site at:
www.sirdar.co.uk

Other useful crochet sites:
www.knitting-and-crochet-guild.co.uk

CREDITS

Quarto would like to thank Vera, at Models Direct, for modelling the garments and Jackie Jones, for make up and hair styling.

All photographs and illustrations are the copyright of Quarto Publishing plc. While every effort has been made to credit contributors, Quarto would like to apologise should there have been any omissions or errors.

Jan Eaton would like to thank Jaeger Handknits, Rowan Yarns and David Rawson at Sirdar for supplying yarns for the projects.